THE BIOGRAPHICAL SCRIPTURE OF KING AŚOKA

BDK English Tripiṭaka 76-II

THE BIOGRAPHICAL SCRIPTURE OF KING AŚOKA

Translated from the Chinese of Saṃghapāla

(Taishō, Volume 50, Number 2043)

by

Li Rongxi

Numata Center
for Buddhist Translation and Research
1993

First Printing, 1993
ISBN: 0-9625618-4-3
Library of Congress Catalog Card Number: 92-082067

Published by
Numata Center for Buddhist Translation and Research
2620 Warring Street
Berkeley, California 94704

Printed in the United States of America

A Message on the Publication of the English Tripiṭaka

The Buddhist canon is said to contain eighty-four thousand different teachings. I believe that this is because the Buddha's basic approach was to prescribe a different treatment for every spiritual ailment, much as a doctor prescribes a different medicine for every medical ailment. Thus his teachings were always appropriate for the particular suffering individual and for the time at which the teaching was given, and over the ages not one of his prescriptions has failed to relieve the suffering to which it was addressed.

Ever since the Buddha's Great Demise over twenty-five hundred years ago, his message of wisdom and compassion has spread throughout the world. Yet no one has ever attempted to translate the entire Buddhist canon into English throughout the history of Japan. It is my greatest wish to see this done and to make the translations available to the many English-speaking people who have never had the opportunity to learn about the Buddha's teachings.

Of course, it would be impossible to translate all of the Buddha's eighty-four thousand teachings in a few years. I have, therefore, had one hundred thirty-nine of the scriptural texts in the prodigious Taishō edition of the Chinese Buddhist canon selected for inclusion in the First Series of this translation project.

It is in the nature of this undertaking that the results are bound to be criticized. Nonetheless, I am convinced that unless someone takes it upon himself or herself to initiate this project, it will never be done. At the same time, I hope that an improved, revised edition will appear in the future.

It is most gratifying that, thanks to the efforts of more than a hundred Buddhist scholars from the East and the West, this monumental project has finally gotten off the ground. May the rays of the Wisdom of the Compassionate One reach each and every person in the world.

NUMATA Yehan
Founder of the English
Tripiṭaka Project

August 7, 1991

Editorial Foreword

In January, 1982, Mr. NUMATA Yehan, the founder of the Bukkyō Dendō Kyōkai (Society for the Promotion of Buddhism), decided to begin the monumental task of the complete translation of the Taishō edition of the Chinese Buddhist canon into the English language. Under his leadership, a special preparatory committee was organized in April, 1982, and by July of the same year the Translation Committee of the English Tripiṭaka (Scriptures) was officially convened.

The initial Committee consisted of the following thirteen members: HANAYAMA Shōyū (Chairman); BANDŌ Shōjun; ISHIGAMI Zennō; KAMATA Shigeo; KANAOKA Shūyū; MAYEDA Sengaku; NARA Yasuaki; SAYEKI Shinkō; (late) SHIOIRI Ryōtatsu; TAMARU Noriyoshi; (late) TAMURA Kwansei; URYŪZU Ryūshin; and YUYAMA Akira. Assistant members of the Committee were as follows: KANAZAWA Atsushi; WATANABE Shōgo; Rolf Giebel of New Zealand; and Rudy Smet of Belgium.

Holding planning meetings on a monthly basis, the Committee has selected one hundred thirty-nine scriptures and texts for the First Series of translations, an estimated one hundred printed volumes in all. Scriptures and texts selected are not necessarily limited to those originally written in India but also include works written or composed in China or Japan. All the volumes in the First Series are scheduled for publication within the twentieth century. While the publication of the First Series proceeds, the scriptures and texts for the Second Series, which is expected to be published in the following ten- or twenty-year period, will be selected from among the remaining works; this process will continue until all the scriptures and texts, in Japanese as well as in Chinese, have been published.

Frankly speaking, it will take perhaps one hundred years or more to accomplish the English translation of the complete

Chinese and Japanese scriptures and texts, which consist of thousands of works. Nevertheless, as Mr. NUMATA wished, it is the sincere hope of the Committee that this project will continue unto completion, even after all its present members have passed away.

It must be mentioned here that the final object of this project is not academic fulfillment but the transmission of the teaching of the Buddha to the whole world in order to create harmony and peace among mankind.

More than eighty Buddhist scholars in the West and in the East, all well qualified to be translators of the Chinese and Japanese scriptures and texts, have agreed to translate certain selected works. It is really a great pleasure for the Committee to announce that more than forty-five translations have already been received as of the end of September, 1992.

The present members of the Translation Committee of the BDK English Tripiṭaka are HANAYAMA Shōyū (Chairman); BANDŌ Shōjun; ISHIGAMI Zennō; ICHISHIMA Shōshin; KAMATA Shigeo; KANAOKA Shūyū; MAYEDA Sengaku; NARA Yasuaki; SAYEKI Shinkō; TAMARU Noriyoshi; URYŪZU Ryūshin; and YUYAMA Akira. Assistant members are WATANABE Shōgo and SUZUKI Kōshin.

Commemorating the ninety-fourth birthday of Mr. NUMATA Yehan, the Committee published the following three texts in a limited edition in April, 1991:

(1) The *Lotus Sutra* (Taishō No. 262)
(2) The *Sutra on Upāsaka Precepts* (Taishō No. 1488)
(3) The *Summary of the Great Vehicle* (Taishō No. 1593)

In December, 1991, the Publication Committee headed by Prof. Philip Yampolsky was organized. New editions of the above volumes and the remaining texts will be published under the supervision of this Committee.

HANAYAMA Shōyū
Chairman
Translation Committee of
the BDK English Tripiṭaka

September 10, 1992

Publisher's Foreword

It was in December, 1991, at the Numata Center for Buddhist Translation and Research in Berkeley, California, that a publication committee was established for the purpose of seeing into print the translations of the Chinese and Japanese Buddhist works in the BDK English Tripiṭaka Series. This committee will perform the duties of copyediting, formatting, proofreading, indexing, consulting with the translators on questionable passages, and so on—the routine duties of any publishing house. Represented on the committee are specialists in Sanskrit, Chinese, and Japanese, who will attempt to ensure that fidelity to the texts is maintained.

This Publication Committee is dedicated to the production of lucid and readable works that will do justice to the vision of Mr. NUMATA Yehan in his desire to make available to Western readers the major works of the Chinese and Japanese Buddhist canon.

"Taishō" refers to the *Taishō Shinshū Daizōkyō* (Newly Revised Tripiṭaka Inaugurated in the Taishō Era), which was published during the period from 1924 to 1934. This consists of one hundred volumes, in which as many as 3,360 scriptures in both Chinese and Japanese are included. This edition is acknowledged to be the most complete Tripiṭaka of the Northern tradition of Buddhism ever published in the Chinese and Japanese languages.

The series number on the spine and title page of each volume will correspond to the number assigned to the work by the Translation Committee of the BDK English Tripiṭaka in Tokyo. A list of the volume numbers is appended at the end of the text. For the convenience of scholars who may wish to turn to the original texts, Taishō page and column numbers are provided in the left-hand margins of each volume. No attempt will be made to standardize the English translations of Buddhist technical terms; these are left to the discretion of the individual translators.

Those participating in the work of this committee are Diane Ames, William Ames, Brian Galloway, David Hall, Nobuo Haneda, and Rev. Seishin Yamashita.

Philip Yampolsky
Chairman
Publication Committee

September 10, 1992

Contents

the Artisan; The Causes of Food and Drink; The Causes of Contentment with Few Desires; The Causes of the Rākṣasas; The Causes of the Tree; The Causes of a Miser; The Causes of the Ghost; The Causes of Being Bitten by Vermin; The Causes of Contemplation on a Skeleton; The Causes of Avarice; The Causes of a Bamboo Brush; The Causes of Parental Sentiment; The Causes of the River; The Causes of a Whim in Meditation; The Causes of the Cowherds; The Causes of the Transformed Person; The Causes of Taking No Delight in the Dwelling Place; The Causes of a Monk's Pewter Staff; The Causes of Sudarśana; The Causes of the Fief for a Monastery; The Causes of Dhītika

Glossary 185

Index 189

A List of the Volumes of the BDK English Tripiṭaka (First Series) 195

Translator's Introduction

In the Chinese Tripiṭaka there are two texts giving legendary accounts of the life of King Aśoka (reigned ca. 265–238 B.C.E. or ca. 273–232 B.C.E.), the third Maurya ruler of Magadha. He was the grandson of Candragupta, the founder of the Maurya dynasty (321–184 B.C.E.), which had its capital at Pāṭaliputra. The first of the texts is the *A-yu-wang-zhuan* (*Aśokāvadāna*) or *Biography of King Aśoka* (Taishō No. 2042), translated into Chinese in seven fascicles by An Faqin, a monk from Anxi (Parthia), who came to Luo-yang in the second year of Tai-kang (281 C.E.) during the reign of Emperor Wu of the Western Jin dynasty. The second text is Saṃghapāla's Chinese translation (512 C.E.) of the *A-yu-wang-jing* (*Aśokarājasūtra*) or *Sutra of King Aśoka* (T. No. 2043) in ten fascicles, upon which the present English translation is based.

In spite of the legendary style of the presentation, this biographical work, of which the original Sanskrit text is little known, gives accounts of the major events in the life of King Aśoka that are historically verifiable through comparative studies of reliable written records and archaeological findings. Although the exact date of the original text is unascertainable, it may be said that it was composed no earlier than 184 B.C.E., when the Maurya dynasty collapsed, because this event is mentioned in the work.

In this work the last king of the Maurya dynasty is given as Puṣyamitra, but according to Brahmanical accounts Puṣyamitra was the name of a general of King Bṛhaddhanus, the last monarch of that dynasty. This general Puṣyamitra is said to have killed the king, usurped the throne, and founded the Śuṅga dynasty in 184 B.C.E.

Besides recounting the major events in the life of King Aśoka, this work devotes half of its space to stories concerning the six patriarchs who succeeded the Buddha in transmitting the Dharma:

Mahākāśyapa, Ānanda, Madhyāntika, Śāṇakavāsin, Upagupta, and Dhītika. It also includes some other stories for the elucidation of the Dharma. Dhītika is unknown to Southern Buddhism and may be looked upon as a hint of the Mahayanist tendency of this work; this hint is enhanced by a sort of short *dhāraṇī* (incantation) in Chinese transliteration in Chapter VIII (which has been restored to the nearest possible romanized Sanskrit by my friend Professor Wu Baihui of the Institute of Philosophy of the Chinese Academy of Social Sciences).

Saṃghapāla (459–524 C.E.), the translator of the Chinese version of the *A-yu-wang-jing*, was a monk from the kingdom of Funan (in the eastern part of present-day Thailand), who came to China during the Qi dynasty (479–501 C.E.) and stayed at Zheng-guan Monastery in the capital, where he studied Mahayana texts under the Indian monk Guṇabhadra and "mastered the languages of several countries" (see *Continued Biographies of Eminent Monks*, Fasc. I, T. No. 2060). When Emperor Wu of the Liang dynasty came to power, he invited Saṃghapāla in the fifth year of Tian-jian (506 C.E.) to translate Buddhist texts into Chinese. In the course of the subsequent seventeen years, he translated eleven Buddhist texts into Chinese, making a total of forty-eight fascicles, including the *A-yu-wang-jing* and the *Vimuktimārga*, with the assistance of Chinese Buddhist monks and lay scholars under imperial patronage. In the fifth year of Pu-tong (524 C.E.), he died of illness at the age of sixty-five at Zheng-guan Monastery.

Li Rongxi

Beijing
June 5, 1987

Chapter I

The Causes of His Birth

131b The Buddha was once staying at Bamboo Grove Monastery in Kalandaka's garden near Rājagṛha. One day he rose early, dressed himself in his robe, and, with a group of *bhikṣus* (mendicants), carried his alms bowl to the city of Rājagṛha to collect alms. At that moment, a *gāthā* (stanza) was heard in the air:

> The Buddha's body is like a golden mountain,
> Walking with the gait of an elephant king.
> So serene and dignified are his features,
> His face resembles the full moon.
> Surrounded by a group of *bhikṣus*,
> He is proceeding to the city.

When the World-honored One had just stepped on the threshold of the gate while he was entering the city, there occurred various miraculous events: the blind recovered their sight, the deaf gained their hearing, the dumb could speak, and the paralyzed could walk; those who were confined in prisons gained liberty and those who bore grudges and hatred became merciful; calves were released spontaneously from their tethers and returned to their mothers; all animals—elephants, horses, cows, and so on—trumpeted, neighed, and mooed aloud with great delight; all birds—parrots, mynas, cuckoos, peacocks, and the like—caroled merrily in concord; all ornaments—rings, bracelets, hairpins, earrings, and all kinds of precious things—clinked melodiously of themselves in their cases; and all musical instruments sounded naturally. At that moment, the earth became clean of itself, free of all sorts of filth, debris, rubble, brambles, and poisonous plants; and it quaked in six ways—when the east rose up the west sank down, when the west rose up the east sank down, when the south rose up the north sank down, when the north rose up the south sank down, when the center rose up the four sides sank down, when the four sides rose up the center sank down, and it all rolled round and round. Such were the wonderful and extraordinary events that happened then. At that moment, another stanza was heard from the air:

> The whole earth depends
> On the four seas,
> With the countries, cities, and mountains
> As its ornaments.
> When the World-honored One trod on the earth,
> It quaked in six ways,
> Like a boat upon the seas
> Blown by a blast of wind.

When the Buddha entered the city, his divine powers caused
131c all the people to dance with delight, like water in the great sea agitated by the wind. All the people uttered the following stanza:

> Of all pleasures in this world,
> None surpasses that of the Buddha entering the country.
> When the earth quakes in six ways,
> All rubble is removed without remnant.
> Those who are imperfect in sense organs
> Become perfect and complete.
> All sorts of musical instruments
> Produce lovely songs by themselves.
> The Buddha's light shines upon all lands
> Like a thousand suns illuminating the world.
> Fragrant water is sprinkled over the ground,
> Which is anointed with powdered sandalwood.
> This city of this country at this moment
> Is the best in decoration and adornment.

At that time the World-honored One walked to the main road, where there were two children, one of whom was the son of an *agrakulika* (one of prominent family) and the other the son of a *kulika* (one of good family). These two children were playing on a heap of sand. The first one was named Jaya and the second one Vijaya. When the two of them saw the Buddha marked on his body with the thirty-two characteristics, the first child put a handful of sand, as if it were cooked rice, into the Buddha's alms bowl. While the second one was rejoicing at this good act with his hands joined palm to palm, the first one uttered the following stanza:

> Endowed with great compassion by nature
> Is this person adorned with a round light
> Who is free from birth and death.
> Now I remember him with one heart.
> As I remember the Buddha in my mind,
> I offer him this handful of sand.

When Jaya had offered the sand, he made a vow, saying, "May I become a *cakravartin* (universal monarch) by the merit of this good root, so that I can make extensive offerings to the Buddha-dharma."

The Buddha knew his mind and saw that his right vow would give rise to a superior and wonderful fruit in a future life. As the Buddha, the Tathāgata, was the field of blessedness, he accepted the sand with a mind of compassion. With a smile, he emitted rays of different colors, blue, yellow, red, and white, either from the top of his head or from below his knees. The rays issuing from below his knees radiated to the eight hells. Those who were suffering in the cold hells felt warmth, and those in the hot ones enjoyed coolness. When the light shone upon their bodies, they were freed from all pains and afflictions. These beings had doubts in their minds: "Now we are free from suffering, but shall we stay here or be born somewhere else?"

At that moment the World-honored One, wishing to arouse good thoughts in them, produced a metamorphic figure and sent it to those beings. Upon seeing the metamorphic figure, they thought in their minds, "Now we shall not be born in other places but are simply liberated from suffering by the power of this person." But the figure made them understand that their retribution in the hells had been dissolved and that they would be born, at the termination of their existence in the hells, in the world of men or in the heavens, where they could realize right views.

The rays issuing from the top of the Buddha's head radiated to
132a the Four Heavenly Kings and up to the highest Akaniṣṭha heaven. In the rays the Buddha expounded the Dharma of suffering, impermanence, voidness, and non-ego, and he also uttered the following stanza:

Be strenuous to become a homeless recluse,
To tally with the Buddha-dharma.
Destroy the army of rebirth
As an elephant shatters a dwelling house.
If a man practices the Buddha-dharma
Diligently and without indolence,
He will be free from birth and death
And gain the cessation of all pain.

The Buddha's light was able to shine upon the whole great chiliocosm and then return to his body. If the Buddha wished to recall past deeds, the light would enter his back; if he wished to predict future events, it would enter his front; if he wished to predict birth in the hells, it would enter his feet; if he wished to predict birth among animals, it would enter his ankles; if he wished to predict birth among the hungry ghosts, it would enter his toes; if he wished to predict birth among mankind, it would enter his knees; if he wished to predict the birth of an iron *cakravartin* king, it would enter his left palm; if he wished to predict the birth of a golden *cakravartin* king, it would enter his right palm; if he wished to predict birth in the heavens, it would enter his navel; if he wished to predict the enlightenment of a *śrāvaka* (a direct disciple of the Buddha), it would enter his mouth; if he wished to predict the enlightenment of a *pratyekabuddha* (a self-enlightened Buddha), it would enter the white curl between his eyebrows; and if he wished to predict the enlightenment of a bodhisattva (a being destined for full Buddhahood), it would enter the protuberance on his head. Each time the light returned from the great chiliocosm, it would first encircle the Buddha three times before it entered the appropriate spots of his body according to circumstances. Now as the Buddha smiled, the light, not without reason, entered his left palm after having encircled him three times.

On seeing this event, Ānanda, with his hands put palm to palm, uttered the following stanza:

> Being free from unrest and arrogance,
> The Buddha turns evils into superior causes.
> He never smiles without a reason,
> Exposing his snow white teeth.
> He knows by his wisdom
> What others are delighted to hear.
> With his supreme, brilliant light,
> He can dissolve others' doubts.
> The Buddha's voice is like thunder;
> His eyes are those of a bull king.
> Being the superior field of blessedness for gods and men,
> He should predict the reward for offering sand.

The Buddha said, "Ānanda, I am not smiling without a reason. There is cause for the Tathāgata, the Worthy and Omniscient One, to wear a smile. Ānanda, did you see the child putting a handful of sand into my alms bowl?" Ānanda said in reply, "Yes, I did." The World-honored One said again, "A hundred years after my nirvana,
132b this child will be born in the city of Pāṭaliputra with the name of Aśoka. He shall be a *cakravartin* king ruling over one of the four continents and take delight in believing the right Dharma. He will build eighty-four thousand stupas to enshrine the Buddha's relic bones for the benefit of many people." The Tathāgata then uttered the following stanza:

> After I have entered nirvana,
> There will be born to the Maurya family
> A king of men named Aśoka,

> Enjoying wide fame for taking delight in the Dharma.
> With stupas containing my relic bones
> He will adorn Jambudvīpa.
> Such will be the reward of the merit
> Gained by offering sand to the Buddha.

The Buddha then took the sand and handed it to Ānanda, saying, "Mix this sand with cow's dung and spread it over the place where the Buddha used to walk in meditation." Ānanda then daubed the ground with the mixture as he was told.

Now in the city of Pāṭaliputra there was a king by the name of Candragupta whose son was Bindusāra; and Bindusāra's eldest son was Susīma.

At that time, a daughter of most elegant features, the best ever known in the country, was born to a Brahman in the city of Campā. A physiognomist said in prediction, "This girl will become a queen and give birth to two sons. The first son will become a *cakravartin* king ruling over one of the four continents, and the second one will be a recluse and attain enlightenment." The Brahman was greatly delighted to hear this prediction.

With a desire to gain wealth and nobility, the Brahman took his daughter to the country of Pāṭaliputra, adorned her with all kinds of ornaments, and sent word to King Bindusāra, "My daughter is most elegant in features, the best ever known in the country. I offer her to the king to be his consort." The king accepted his offer and kept the girl in his harem. His other consorts in the harem, however, considered the matter among themselves, saying, "This girl is the most elegant in the country. If the king sees her, he will certainly be attracted by her beauty and will love us no more." Thinking in this way, the royal consorts ordered the girl to serve the king as his barber.

Once the king ordered a shave, and while the girl was shaving him he fell asleep. When he woke up he was pleased with the girl and said to her, "Whatever you wish to have, you may declare it." Then the girl said to the king, "I wish to have enjoyment with Your Majesty." The king said, "As you are a barber and I am a king, how can I enjoy you?" The girl replied to the king, "I am the daughter of a Brahman and not a barber. My father, a Brahman, intended me to be the king's consort." The king inquired, "Who has made you a barber?" "The royal consorts," was the reply. The king said again, "You need not do this job any more." And he took the girl to be his consort.

132c Shortly afterwards she became pregnant, and ten months later she gave birth to a son. As the king thought that he had no sorrow, he named his son Aśoka (No Sorrow). As his second son was born at a time when he was without sorrow, he named the child Vītaśoka (Without Sorrow). Aśoka was rough and coarse in appearance, and his father did not like him.

At that time, King Bindusāra wished to know through physiognomy which of his sons was competent to succeed him on the throne. So he summoned a heretical physiognomist named Piṅgalavatsājīva, to whom he said, "Venerable teacher, I wish to know through physiognomy which of my sons is competent to succeed me as king after my death." Piṅgalavatsājīva said in reply, "If Your Majesty wishes to read the future of the princes, we should go to the Golden Palace." King Bindusāra then took the princes to the Golden Palace.

Aśoka's mother said to him, "Today His Majesty wishes to read the future of the princes. You may go to join them." Aśoka said, "As the king does not like me, why should I go?" His mother said, "Just go." Aśoka said in reply, "I shall go as you order me. But please ask somebody to send my food to that place."

When Aśoka was leaving the city of Pāṭaliputra, he met a minister of the court by the name of Rādhagupta, who asked Aśoka, "Where do you intend to go?" Aśoka said in reply, "Today the king is at the Golden Palace in order to read the future of the princes. I am going there." Rādhagupta then handed his good old elephant to Aśoka so that he could ride to the Golden Palace. After arriving at that place, Aśoka sat down on the ground among the other princes, who all had various kinds of food and drink contained in golden and silver vessels. Aśoka's mother prepared rice and cream, which she put in an earthenware vessel and sent to him.

King Bindusāra said to the physiognomist, "You should read the future of the princes one by one to see who is competent to be king after my death." The physiognomist pondered over the matter in his mind, thinking, "If I say Aśoka is competent to be king, the king will certainly kill me, because he does not value him." Having considered the matter in this way, the physiognomist said to the king, "For certain reasons I shall not mention any name in my physiognomic reading." The king said, "Good." Then the physiognomist said, "The prince who has the best animal for riding will be competent to be king." The king said, "Go on with your prediction." The physiognomist said again, "The prince who is sitting on the best seat will be competent to be king." The king said again, "Go on with your prediction." The physiognomist said again, "The prince who has the best food and drink contained in the best vessels will be competent to be king."

When the princes heard these words, each of them thought that he had the best animal for riding, the best seat, and the best food and drink contained in the best vessels, and that he should be king. But Aśoka thought in his mind, "Now this physiognomist refuses to mention any name in his physiognomic reading. If the one who has the best riding animal will be competent to be king,
133a then I have the best riding animal. I have the great earth as my seat; and I eat rice and cream, the best of foods. My vessel is made of earth, and what I drink is water. So far as I can see, I shall be king."

The physiognomist paid a visit to [Aśoka's] mother, who asked him, "Who will become king after the demise of His Majesty?" He said in reply, "Aśoka." [Aśoka's] mother then said to the physiognomist, "If the king inquires any more about who is competent to be king, you should go to a distant place and not stay here. But you may come back when Aśoka becomes king." So the physiognomist went far away to some other country.

At that time, a country named Takṣaśilā, which was under the rule of King Bindusāra, attempted to rebel against his suzerainty. King Bindusāra said to Aśoka, "You may assemble the four divisions of troops and march to that country." But no weapons or provisions were given to him. When Aśoka was leaving the city of Pāṭaliputra with the four divisions of troops under his command, they asked him, "Now as we have no weapons or provisions, how can we go to subdue that country?" Aśoka said, "If I am meritorious and deserve to be king, weapons and provisions should come out by themselves." No sooner had he uttered these words than a gap opened in the earth, from which weapons and provisions emerged. Thus Aśoka, commanding the four divisions of troops, went to punish Takṣaśilā.

Upon hearing that Aśoka was coming, the people of Takṣaśilā came out half a *yojana* [one *yojana* is a day's journey in an ox cart] to decorate the road and sprinkle scented water over the ground to receive Aśoka, to whom they said, "We come to welcome you, O Prince, not to fight with you, nor do we harbor any enmity against His Majesty the great king. But the minister sent by the king is governing our country in a bad way, and we wish that he be recalled." Then the people offered various gifts to Aśoka and welcomed him to their country, as has been extensively related.

Aśoka was again sent by the king as an envoy to the country of Kāśī. In the country of Kāśī there were two warriors, who said to their king, "We two are strong enough to level a mountain. When Aśoka comes we need not serve him as his subjects." At that moment, the heavenly beings voiced a warning, saying, "Aśoka will be a *cakravartin* king to rule over one of the four continents. You should not go against him."

Now Susīma, the eldest son of King Bindusāra, was returning from the royal gardens to the city of Pāṭaliputra when he met on the way the king's prime minister, who was bald, coming out of the city. To joke with him, Susīma patted him on his bald crown. The prime minister thought, "Even now he dared to pat me on the head. Should he become king, he would certainly hurt me with a sword. It befits me to take measures to prevent him from becoming king." Thus he ordered five hundred ministers to leave Susīma, and he announced that Aśoka would be a *cakravartin* king ruling over one of the four continents and that all of them should serve

133b him together. He even agitated the people of Takṣaśilā to rebel against the king, refusing to be his subjects any more.

King Bindusāra dispatched Susīma to subjugate the rebels, but when he reached that country he could not suppress the revolt. At that time Aśoka returned home, and King Bindusāra, who was seriously ill and on his deathbed, ordered a messenger to instruct Aśoka to go back to Takṣaśilā, while asking Susīma to return home speedily, saying, "I intend to hand over state affairs to him."

The ministers smeared Aśoka's body with the yellow juice of ginger to make him look as if he were sick, and they also boiled *lākṣā* (red dye) and kept the juice in a bowl, which they put someplace, while announcing that Aśoka was ill.

When King Bindusāra was approaching his end, the ministers dressed Aśoka and took him to the king, to whom they said, "This is a prince. Your Majesty ought to give him the throne. When Susīma returns, we shall restore the throne to him."

Upon hearing these words, the king was greatly enraged. Aśoka said, "If I am the legal king, let the heavenly beings crown me right now." When he had said so, the heavenly beings immediately put a celestial crown on his head. At this sight, the king was all the more furious and died with hot blood oozing from his mouth.

Then Aśoka ascended the throne; and after ascending the throne he appointed Rādhagupta as his prime minister.

Susīma was very angry to hear that Aśoka had ascended the throne after the death of the king, and he wished to punish Aśoka with his troops. Aśoka, in his city, mobilized a great number of soldiers to guard the four gates of the city. He ordered two strong and valorous generals with groups of soldiers to guard the southern and western gates; he ordered his prime minister Rādhagupta with a group of soldiers to guard the northern gate; and he himself, commanding a group of soldiers, guarded the eastern gate. Rādhagupta made by different expedients various kinds of devices at the eastern gate of the city; he had figures of Aśoka and his soldiers carved out of wood and had ditches dug in the ground in which smokeless fires were kept burning under coverings that were camouflaged by dry earth scattered over them.

Susīma and his troops intended to attack the northern gate, but Rādhagupta said to him, "Don't attack me. You should attack the eastern gate. If you can kill King Aśoka, I will surrender to you." Listening to his suggestion, Susīma directed his army to attack the eastern gate, where, seeing that none of the wooden figures was moving, he marched straight forward, fell into the fire pits, and burned to death.

After Susīma's death, his army commander, Bhadrayudha by
133c name, a brave and powerful man, led his army of more than a thousand soldiers to become Buddhist monks to practice the Way; and they attained arhatship (sainthood).

King Aśoka administered state affairs, but his five hundred ministers disdained him. Once he said to his ministers, "Pull up flower and fruit trees to protect thorns and brambles." The ministers said in reply, "No! We should pull up thorns and brambles to protect flower and fruit trees." But Aśoka repeated that they should pull up flower and fruit trees to protect thorns and brambles. Three times his ministers disobeyed him. In a fit of anger, Aśoka drew his sword and beheaded the five hundred ministers.

Another time, King Aśoka took five hundred maids of honor to the rear garden, where there was a tree with profuse flowers and foliage called an *aśoka* tree. On seeing this tree, King Aśoka said, "I am glad that this tree bears the same name as I."

As Aśoka was physically rough and coarse, the maids did not wish to go near him. While he was sleeping in the garden, the maids, intending to displease him, plucked all the flowers and leaves of the tree, leaving it bare. When Aśoka woke up and saw the bare tree, he asked the maids, "Who stripped this tree so completely?" The maids said in reply, "We did it." In a fit of anger, King Aśoka wrapped all the maids in bamboo screens and burned them to death. As he was so wicked, the people of the time called him Caṇḍāśoka (Cruel Aśoka).

The prime minister Rādhagupta told King Caṇḍāśoka that he should not personally beat or kill but should order somebody else to do it. Thus the king recruited an executioner. There lived then in a village in the mountains a man good at weaving clothes, who had a son called by his father Girika. This young man was so fearsome that he was capable of doing unrighteous deeds and always scolded his parents. He beat everyone, male or female, in the household and would kill or hurt all living creatures. His trade was fishing and hunting, and as he did so much slaughtering, he was also called by the people Caṇḍagirika.

When the king was searching for a cruel person, [his messenger] came upon this man. The messenger said to him, "The king wishes to govern the people by means of killing. Can you do the job?" The man answered, "I could kill everybody in the whole of Jambudvīpa, if I were asked to do so." The messenger reported to the king what the man had said, and the king ordered that he be brought to his presence. By order of the king, the messenger went to the man's place and told him, "The king has asked you to come." The man said to the messenger, "Just wait a moment. I must go to see my parents." Then he went to inform his parents that King Aśoka wished to govern the people by means of killing, that he had asked him to do the job, and that he was willing
134a to go. But his parents would not permit him to go; and so in a fit of rage, he murdered his parents. Then he returned to the messenger, who asked him, "Why are you so late?" The man said in reply, "Because my parents would not allow me to go, I finished them off."

When the man came to the palace, he told the king that if he wished to punish people, he should build a prison with a gate well decorated to look most magnificent, so that anybody who saw it would be delighted with it. He also asked the king to issue a strict order that nobody should be allowed to come out once he had entered the prison. The king said, "Very good."

Caṇḍagirika then went to Kukkuṭa Monastery, where a *bhikṣu* was reciting a scripture in which the events in the hells were related, such as cauldrons with boiling water, furnaces with burning charcoal, mountains planted with knives, trees bearing swords, and other painful implements of punishment. Those who were born in the hells were punished according to the sins they had committed. Such hellish things were extensively related in the *Scripture of the Five Divine Lictors*. Upon hearing these words, Caṇḍagirika made all the implements of torture that were used in the hells.

In the country of Śrāvastī, there was a merchant who went to sea with his wife; a son was born to them while they were at sea, and the child was thus named Sāgara (Sea). After voyaging to and fro for twelve years, they encountered five hundred pirates, who killed the merchant and seized his property. His son alone escaped death. Later he became a Buddhist monk, and on his wanderings he reached the country of Pāṭaliputra. One day he got up early, dressed himself properly, and went into the country with alms bowl in hand to collect food. As he did not know the place, he entered the prison to beg for alms, because he saw that its gate was so nicely decorated. Inside the prison he saw all kinds of implements of torture and intended to withdraw. But Caṇḍagirika got hold of him and said, "You shall suffer death and cannot go out." Being frightened, the monk cried and wept with tears flowing down. Caṇḍagirika said to him, "Why are you crying like a child?" The monk replied, "It is not because I value my body, but because it is difficult to attain emancipation. It is difficult to renounce one's home, but this I did. It is difficult to live during the time of Śākyamuni Buddha, but I am living in it. I have not gained the true Dharma of all Dharmas, and that is why I am anxious and worried." Caṇḍagirika said to the monk, "I have been instructed by the great king that nobody should be allowed to leave this prison once he has come into it." The monk said with tears, "You must allow me one month's extension." "Not one month, but seven days may be allowed," was the reply. Considering that he was approaching his death, the monk zealously practiced the Dharma with great energy for the full seven days.

At that time, a prince had a talk with a palace maid, and King Aśoka, being irritated by the sight, had the two of them sent to the prison for punishment. Caṇḍagirika put them in an iron mortar and pounded them with a pestle. Greatly terrified by the sight, the
134b monk uttered the following stanza:

The Great Master, the Buddha compassionate,
The Leading Recluse, has rightly said that
This material form is like a bubble,
Unsubstantial and not ever-abiding.
This fair and graceful body—
Where is it after its destruction?
Thus one should give up
What the ignorant take pleasure in.
I should realize that on this occasion.
I shall gain liberation in this prison.
With its aid I shall cross
The sea of the three realms of being.

In that one night the monk meditated with full energy and attained arhatship after cutting off his passions. Caṇḍagirika said to him, "The night is over and the day is dawning. You should know that the time of suffering is approaching." The monk said in reply, "I do not know what you mean by saying that the night is over and the day is dawning. But I do realize that the night of ignorance is over and the sun of wisdom is appearing. By the light of the sun of wisdom, I see that nothing has reality in this world. Thus I intend to edify the world with the Dharma of the Buddha." He also told Caṇḍagirika, "Now you may do whatever you please with this body of mine."

At that time, the warden of the prison, being a merciless man and having seen nothing of the world, relentlessly put the monk into an iron cauldron, poured pus, blood, feces, urine, and other filthy things into it, and built a big fire with much fuel to boil the monk in the cauldron. But when the fuel was exhausted, the body of the monk was not damaged at all. On seeing that the monk's shape was not changed, the warden beat and scolded the jailors angrily, "Why don't you add more fuel to the fire?"

The warden then personally added fuel to the fire, but it would not burn. Meanwhile he saw that the monk was sitting cross-legged on a lotus flower in the cauldron. After seeing this phenomenon, the warden immediately went to report to the king.

Upon hearing this matter, the king, followed by his people, went to see it. At that moment the monk instantly came out of the iron cauldron by his supernatural powers and rose up into the air like a king goose hovering in the air in eighteen different ways.

King Aśoka was delighted to see the monk as conspicuous as a mountain appearing in the air, and he uttered the following stanza:

Your body is similar to that of an ordinary man,
But your divine powers surpass the ability of men.
I do not know about this:
Who are you in fact?
You should tell me the truth
And let me know you now.
If I know the truth,
I shall be a disciple of yours.

134c The monk then thought in his mind, "This king is now capable of accepting the Buddha's words. He will build many stupas to enshrine the Buddha's relics, so that all people can gain the benefit of the Dharma." Having thought so, he wished to reveal the Buddha's merits and uttered the following stanza:

The Buddha has cut off all passions;
His great compassion is incomparable.
I am a disciple
Of the best debater of the highest grade.
The inexhaustible power of the right Dharma
Regards nothing as a real being.
The Buddha is a bull king among men
Who can control himself and regulate others.
It is he who has liberated me
From the prison of the three realms of being.

[And he said,] "The king was also predicted by the Buddha, 'A hundred years after my nirvana, there will be a king by the name of Aśoka in the city of Pāṭaliputra. He will be a *cakravartin* king and rule over one of the four continents, and he will construct eighty-four thousand stupas for the enshrinement of my relics.

The prison to be built by the king, in which numerous people will be killed, will be like the hells. He will finally demolish it and impart freedom from fear to all living beings.' The great king should now comply with the Buddha's wishes." He then uttered the following stanza:

> Thus the great king of men
> Should have a mind of pity
> For all living beings
> And grant them freedom from fear.
> Complying with the wishes of the World-honored One,
> He should erect numerous stupas for his relics.

King Aśoka, fixing his mind on the Buddha and putting his hands palm to palm, uttered the following stanza in penitence:

> I take refuge in the Buddha, the Dharma,
> And his disciples in the Sangha (Buddhist Order).
> May you, the son of the ten powers,
> Treat me with patience.
> All the evils that I have done
> I shall confess to you.
> Now I shall cultivate my mind with diligence
> And with a mind of deep veneration.
> I shall decorate this earth
> With many types of Buddha-stupas
> As white as snow and jade,
> To conform with the Buddha's augury.

The monk exclaimed in reply, "Excellent!" and then returned by supernatural powers to his own place.

When King Aśoka was about to leave the prison, Caṇḍagirika said to him, with his hands joined palm to palm, "Your Majesty is aware that I have been instructed not to allow anybody to go out of this prison once he has entered it." The king said to him, "Do you intend to kill me?" "Yes," was the reply. The king asked him, "Which of us came in first?" Caṇḍagirika said in reply, "I came in
135a first." Then the king told the jailors to arrest Caṇḍagirika, put him

in the *lakuca* (glue) house, and set it on fire. He also ordered people to demolish the prison so as to impart freedom from fear to all living beings.

With the intention of building numerous Buddha-stupas, the king arrayed his four divisions of troops and went to the Droṇa Stupa constructed by King Ajātaśatru. Upon arriving at the stupa, he ordered his men to pull it down and take out the relics buried in it. In this way he took out the relics from seven stupas one after another. Then he went to a village named Rāmagrāma, where stood the first stupa ever built. He intended to break it also and take out the relics.

The Nāga king then invited Aśoka to the Nāga palace and said to him, "This is the stupa to which I always make offerings. May Your Majesty preserve it." King Aśoka consented, and then the Nāga king sent him back to Rāmagrāma. Considering that the Nāga king protected that stupa with twice the usual attention because it was the first one ever built in the world, Aśoka realized that he could not obtain the relics contained therein and returned to his own country.

King Aśoka made eighty-four thousand precious cases and put the relics in all of them. He also made eighty-four thousand vases, banners, and canopies and gave them to the Yakṣas (devils), ordering them to erect stupas at all places on earth and even over the great seas. He also announced that if any country in one of the three categories—the small, the medium, or the large ones—paid the sum of one crore of taels of gold, one royal stupa would be built there. Now as the country of Takṣaśilā paid thirty-six crores of taels of gold, its people said to King Aśoka, "May Your Majesty give us thirty-six cases."

Upon hearing these words, the king wondered how, since he intended to build numerous stupas at all places, this country could be allowed to obtain so many cases of relics. Thus he said expediently to the people of that country, "Now I shall exempt you from thirty-five crores of taels of gold." And he also declared, "From now onwards, all countries, whether they have more or fewer stupas, will not have to pay me any more gold."

King Aśoka then went to the great virtuous arhat Yaśas, to whom he said, "I wish to complete the construction of all of the eighty-four thousand stupas in one moment in one day." And he uttered the following stanza:

> I took from the first seven stupas
> The relics of the World-honored One.
> A king of the Maurya family am I,
> Constructing stupas in one day,
> Eighty-four thousand in number,
> As brilliant as white clouds.

Having erected eighty-four thousand stupas, King Aśoka supported and protected the Buddha-dharma, so much so that the people of the time called him Dharmāśoka. All the people uttered the following stanza:

> 135b The great holy king of the Maurya family,
> Knowing that the Dharma is of great benefit,
> Dotted the world with many stupas
> And gave up his ill fame on earth.
> Having gained the good name of a Dharma King,
> By the Dharma he has achieved happiness.

End of Fascicle One
of the *Biographical Scripture of King Aśoka*

The above was translated by Saṃghapāla, a *śramaṇa* (Buddhist monk) of Funan, on the twentieth day of the sixth month in the eleventh year of Tian-jian (512 C.E.) of the Liang dynasty at the Shou-guang Hall in Yang-du. See Baochang's *New Catalogue of Chinese Buddhist Texts*.

Chapter II

The Causes of Seeing Upagupta

When King Aśoka had constructed eighty-four thousand relic stupas, he was very glad, and together with his ministers he went to Kukkuṭa Monastery. Upon arriving at the monastery, he went to the abbot to salute him with his hands joined palm to palm and said, "The Buddha, who was the All-seer, predicted that I would receive my present reward as a result of my offering a handful of sand to him. Was there any other person to whom the Buddha said anything in prediction?" The chief *bhikṣu* of the time was named Yaśas, who answered King Aśoka in the affirmative. Before the World-honored One entered nirvana, there were a Nāga king named Apalāla and a potter as well as a *caṇḍāla* (wicked) Nāga king. After having converted them, the Buddha came to the country of Mathurā. In Mathurā he told the Elder Ānanda, "A hundred years after the nirvana of the Tathāgata, there will be in this country of Mathurā a perfumer by the name of Gupta, who will have a son named Upagupta. Being a Buddha without the characteristic marks on his body, Upagupta will edify the people in a most excellent way and perform a Buddha's functions after my nirvana." He also said to Ānanda, "Do you see yonder green forest?" Ānanda replied, "Yes, I see it." The Buddha said, "There is a mountain over there called Urumaṇḍa. A hundred years after the nirvana of the Tathāgata, a monastery with the name Naṭabhaṭikā will be built on the mountain; it will be the best place for meditation." The World-honored One then uttered the following stanza:

Among all the learned disciples,
The best in wisdom,

As the World-honored One prophesied,
Is the one named Upagupta.
This great virtuous one in this world
Will widely perform the Buddha's functions.

135c King Aśoka inquired of the abbot Yaśas, "Has Upagupta been born or not?" The great virtuous Yaśas said in reply, "He has been born and is now on Urumaṇḍa Mountain. He is free from all passions, and various arhats are following him to gather up and save all suffering beings in the world. Thus he is preaching the Dharma, as the All-wise One, to Devas, human beings, and Asuras as well as Nāgas and divine beings."

At that time, the Elder Upagupta, surrounded by eighteen thousand arhats, was at Naṭabhaṭikā Monastery. King Aśoka uttered the following stanza to his ministers:

Quickly make arrangements to mobilize
My army of elephants, horses, chariots, and footmen.
I intend to go to that country
Where stands the mountain Urumaṇḍa,
To see the Great Virtuous One
With the name of Upagupta.
Through diligent cultivation to end his passions,
He has reached the stage of an arhat in perfection.

The ministers said to King Aśoka, "Let Your Majesty just send a messenger to tell the people there to ask Upagupta to come to the king." But the king said in reply, "He is an arhat. We should not despise or humiliate him but should go in person to salute him." And he uttered the following stanza:

Living in the world like a Tathāgata
Is the one whose name is Upagupta.
If one receives not his commands,
His heart is made of adamant.

King Aśoka then sent a messenger to Upagupta to inform him, "We wish to come to the Great Virtuous One." Upon hearing this message, Upagupta thought, "If King Aśoka comes here, he will certainly bring with him a large retinue that would cause much loss to this country." Then he said to the messenger, "I will go to him. There is no need for the king to come here."

Thus the king built ships to welcome Upagupta and repaired all the roads leading to the country of Mathurā. At that time, Upagupta and his eighteen thousand arhats embarked for Pāṭaliputra with the intention of converting the king to the teachings of the Buddha.

A subject of King Aśoka said to him, "It is for the sake of converting Your Majesty that Upagupta is coming to this country. It befits Your Majesty to know that the Buddha-dharma is comparable to a ship, by which you will be able, as you have cultivated goodness, to ferry across the sea of the three realms of existence and reach the other shore of non-action. Early tomorrow morning, Upagupta will walk to Your Majesty."

Being delighted to hear these words, the king untied his string of pearls, worth a crore of taels of gold, and awarded it to the man. He also ordered the man to make an announcement with the beating of a drum, so that all people in Pāṭaliputra might know
136a that Upagupta was coming on the following day. The man was also instructed to utter the following stanza:

> Those who wish to enjoy the bliss of riches,
> Be born in the heavens, or achieve the causes of liberation,
> Should all go to see
> That person Upagupta.
> One who did not see the Buddha—
> The most honored one among bipedal beings,
> Who was compassionate by intrinsic nature,
> The great master free from passions—
> Should go with offerings
> To see the person named Upagupta.

King Aśoka made all his people hear this stanza and also ordered them to mend and decorate the roads. He went out of the city to a distance of half a *yojana*, together with his subjects, holding flowers and playing various musical instruments, to welcome

Upagupta. On seeing that Upagupta had already come ashore at a distance, surrounded by eighteen thousand arhats standing in a group shaped like a crescent moon, King Aśoka alighted from his elephant and walked to Upagupta. With one foot on board the ship and the other one on land, he carried Upagupta in his hands onto the ship, where he prostrated himself, with his knees, elbows, and head touching the floor, at the feet of the monk, like a big tree collapsing on the earth. After kissing the monk's feet, he knelt before him, put his hands palm to palm, and gazed at him with admiration while he uttered the following stanza:

The earth has the sea as its garment
With mountains as canopies for its adornment.
Being rid of my foes I obtained this earth,
Which makes me feel delighted.
More am I delighted today
To meet you, the Most Virtuous One.
As I see you today,
I feel doubly happy in my mind.
It is like seeing the World-honored One.
This is why I am happy in my mind.
Though the Buddha has entered nirvana,
You, the Most Virtuous One, are performing his functions.
In the darkness of the world,
You are the light of the sun and moon.
You adorn the world with wisdom,
As the Great Master has done.
The best person for the edification of men,
You are the shelter for all living beings.
May you give me instruction and
I shall act according to your teachings.

Upagupta, the Most Virtuous One, stroked Aśoka's head with his right hand and uttered the following stanza:

Although Your Majesty is now free from obstacles,
You should still practice non-slackness.
It is rare to meet the Three Treasures,

To which offerings should always be made.
136b The World-honored One transmitted the Dharma-*piṭaka*
To you, to me, and to others.
The Buddha-dharma you should constantly guard,
In order to convert all living beings.

King Aśoka said in reply, "I have done what the World-honored One predicted." And he also uttered the following stanza:

Offerings have I made to the relics
Of the World-honored One and to his statues.
Stupas have been built at all places,
Decorated with gems and jewels.
The only thing I cannot do is to renounce
My home for the pure life of a recluse.

Upagupta said, "It is excellent, really excellent that Your Majesty has done such things, which are worthy of being done by a king. And why?"

Your Majesty should practice reality
With your body, life, and property.
If you are reborn in another world,
You will not suffer pains in that world.

Offering a large amount of gifts to Upagupta, King Aśoka brought him to the city and carried the Most Virtuous One to a high seat. Upagupta's body was as soft and smooth as cotton; and the king, having touched his body, uttered the following stanza with his hands joined palm to palm:

Your body is soft and smooth,
Like silk and cotton.
My rough and coarse body
Has touched Your Reverence.

Upagupta then uttered the following stanza:

I have offered the best gift
To the Buddha, the World-honored One.

> It was unlike the sand
> You presented to the Tathāgata.

King Aśoka again uttered the following stanza:

> I had the mind of a child,
> To offer sand to the World-honored One
> Who was the field of blessedness.
> Thus I have become a king.

In order to please Aśoka, Upagupta uttered the following stanza:

> Your Majesty met the field of blessedness
> In which grew the seeds of giving alms.
> Hence you gained the reward
> Of wonderful happiness.

Having heard this stanza, the king felt greatly pleased and uttered the following stanza:

> Formerly I offered sand to the World-honored One,
> The field of great blessedness.
> Now I have gained incomparable happiness,
> Being a quarter of a *cakravartin* king.
> Who, upon hearing of this event,
> Will not make offerings to the Tathāgata?

136c At that time, King Aśoka worshipped at Upagupta's feet and said, "Most Virtuous One, I wish to make offerings to all the places where the Buddha walked, stood, sat, or lay. I also wish to mark the places to let the people of the future know where the Buddha, the Tathāgata, walked, stood, sat, or lay, so that they may be converted to the teachings of the Buddha." Then he uttered the following stanza:

> I intend to make offerings
> To all places where the Tathāgata
> Walked, stood, sat, or lay,
> So that I may be free from the pains of rebirth.
> I also wish to make images of the Tathāgata

Walking, standing, sitting, or lying,
To provide people of the future
With a chance of seeing the Buddha.

Upagupta said in reply, "It is excellent, Your Majesty, really excellent! This intention of yours is most difficult to realize. Now I shall show you the places of the four postures of the Tathāgata, the World-honored One, so that you can make images for the purpose of converting all living beings."

At that time, King Aśoka arrayed his four divisions of troops, holding flowers and playing music, and went with Upagupta to those places. Upagupta took King Aśoka to the Buddha's birthplace in the wood of Luṃbinī, and said with his right hand pointing to the place, "King Aśoka, this is the Buddha's birthplace." And then he uttered the following stanza:

This is the first place of the World-honored One,
Where he walked seven steps after he was born.
With pure eyes he observed the four quarters
And made a Lion's Roar, saying,
"This is my last birth
From a mother's womb."

King Aśoka prostrated himself on the ground to worship the place where the Tathāgata was born and uttered the following stanza with his hands joined palm to palm:

One who has seen the Buddha
Possesses great merits.
If one has heard the Lion's Roar,
He gains the same merits.

In order to engender a mind of deep faith in King Aśoka, Upagupta asked him, "Do you wish to see a heavenly being who saw the Buddha walking seven steps after he was born and heard the Lion's Roar?" The king said in reply, "Most Virtuous One, I do wish to see him." Upagupta said, "The heavenly being is residing on the branch that Mahāmāyā was holding when the Tathāgata was born." Then he pointed to the place and uttered the following stanza:

> If there is any heavenly being
> Residing in this wood,
> Who has seen the World-honored One
> And heard his Lion's Roar,
> May he appear in person
> To engender Aśoka's conviction.

137a The heavenly being then appeared in person and stood with hands joined palm to palm before Upagupta, to whom he said, "Most Virtuous One, what do you wish me to do?"

Upagupta said to King Aśoka, "This heavenly being saw the Buddha at the time of his birth." With his hands joined palm to palm, King Aśoka uttered the following stanza to the heavenly being:

> You saw the Buddha when he was born
> With a dignified body of a hundred blisses.
> His features resembled a lotus flower,
> Loved and admired by the whole world.
> You also heard the Lion's Roar
> Right in this great wood.

The heavenly being uttered the following stanza in reply:

> I have seen the Buddha's body,
> Brilliant with golden hues,
> Walking seven steps in air,
> The supreme one among all bipeds.
> The Lion's Roar I also heard,
> Honored by heavenly beings and mankind.

The king inquired, "What were the auspicious signs when the Tathāgata was born?" The heavenly being answered, "It is not possible for me to relate all the wonderful things in full. I can tell only a few things briefly." Then he uttered the following stanza:

> Emitting a light of golden color,
> Shining upon this blind world,

He was adored by men and beings in heavens,
And the earth quaked with the sea and mountains.

King Aśoka offered a hundred thousand taels of gold to the birthplace of the Tathāgata, where he constructed a stupa. Then he went to the other places.

Upagupta took King Aśoka to the abode of a recluse in Kapilavastu and pointed to the place to show the king. It was at this place that the Bodhisattva, as an infant with a lovely body well adorned with the thirty-two physical marks, was shown to King Śuklodana. On seeing that place, King Aśoka prostrated himself on the ground to worship it. Śākyavardhana was a place of divine beings. When the Bodhisattva went there to pay homage to the divine beings, they declined to accept his worship but saluted him. When King Śuklodana witnessed this event, he remarked, "This son of mine is the Deva of Devas." Thus he was called Devātideva.

Upagupta said again, "This is the place where the Brahman physiognomist read the features of the Bodhisattva." He also said, "This is the place where a recluse predicted the Bodhisattva's future, saying that the child would become a Buddha." He also said, "This is the place where Mahāprajāpatī fostered the Bodhisattva." He also said, "This is the place where the Bodhisattva studied books." He also said, "This is the place where the Bodhisattva learned the arts of riding an elephant, a chariot, and a horse." He also said, "This is the place where the Bodhisattva fully mastered different arts and crafts." He also said, "This
137b is the place where the Bodhisattva turned the Wheel of the Dharma." He also said, "This is the place where he amused himself with sixty thousand maids of honor." He also said, "This is the place where the Bodhisattva felt sorry at the sight of an aged man, a sick person, and a corpse." He also said, "This is the place where the Bodhisattva practiced meditation and other methods for getting rid of desire and evils under a *jambu* tree. Here he gained enlightenment and insight and entered the first stage of *dhyāna* (trance), in which he was freed from rebirth

and enjoyed bliss. While the Bodhisattva was sitting in meditation the sun passed the meridian, but the shadow of the tree under which he was sitting did not move, whereas the shadows of other trees shifted as the sun moved. At this sight, King Śuklodana prostrated himself on the ground to worship at the Bodhisattva's feet. Ten thousand heavenly beings of that place attended the Bodhisattva and followed him going out of the city of Kapilavastu at midnight." Again, there was the place where the Bodhisattva took off his precious crown and sent his horse and the groom Chandaka back home. The following stanza was uttered:

> His precious crown and pearls were forsaken,
> Together with his horse and Chandaka,
> Whom he sent back to his homeland.
> Proceeding alone without a guard,
> To cultivate himself with effort,
> He entered the mountains to learn the Way.

At this place the Bodhisattva gave his silk garment to a hunter in exchange for his robe and became a homeless recluse.

This was the place where Bhārgava invited the Bodhisattva. This was the place where King Bimbisāra offered half of his kingdom to the Bodhisattva. This was the place where he studied under Udraka Rāmaputra. The following stanza was then uttered:

> At this place there was a recluse,
> Whose name was Udraka Rāmaputra.
> Going away after hearing his dharma,
> The King of Men had no more teachers.

At this place he practiced asceticism for six years. The following stanza was also uttered:

> For six years of ascetic life,
> I did what was hard to do.
> Knowing that austerity was not the Way,
> I gave up the recluse's practice.

This was the place where the Bodhisattva accepted the milk congee prepared with milk collected from sixteen cows and offered by the two maids Nandā and Nandabalā. The following stanza was uttered:

> It was at this place that the Bodhisattva
> Took Nandā's offering of milk congee.
> The Great Hero, whose words were supreme,
> From here went to the Bodhi tree.

At this place the Nāga king Kālika eulogized the Bodhisattva, as was stated in the following stanza:

> The Nāga king named Kālika
> Said in commendation:
> "By this way he will go
> To the Bodhi tree."

At that time, King Aśoka worshipped at the feet of Upagupta and,
with his hands joined palm to palm, said to him, "I wish to see the
137c Nāga king who has formerly seen the Tathāgata walking like an
elephant king, going by this way to the Bodhi tree." Upagupta then
went to the abode of Kālika and uttered the following stanza while
he pointed at the Nāga king:

> The most eminent of all Nāga kings,
> May you appear in your true form,
> As you saw the Bodhisattva
> Going from here to the Bodhi tree.

Then the Nāga king Kālika appeared in his physical form, stood before Upagupta with his hands joined palm to palm, and said, "Most Virtuous One, what do you wish me to do?" Upagupta said to King Aśoka, "This is the Nāga king Kālika, who praised the Bodhisattva when he was going by this way to the Bodhi tree." King Aśoka put his hands palm to palm and uttered the following stanza to the Nāga king Kālika:

> You have seen the Buddha, the World-honored One,
> Whose light was of a golden hue.

None was comparable to him in this world.
His face was like the full moon in autumn.
Of the great merits of his ten powers
Please say just one portion.
How did he go from here,
The Buddha who possessed divine powers?

The Nāga king Kālika said in reply, "It is impossible for me to relate all this in full, but I will tell you briefly. May Your Majesty listen to me." Then he uttered the following stanza:

When the Bodhisattva walked on the earth,
It quaked in six ways.
The great sea and mountains
Issued a light brighter than the sun.

After having constructed a stupa at the place of the Nāga king, King Aśoka went away to other places.

Upagupta then took King Aśoka to the Bodhi tree and pointed to it, saying, "Your Majesty, this is the place where the Bodhisattva, accompanied by compassion, conquered the army of Māra and attained the supreme perfect enlightenment." He also uttered the following stanza:

It was here that the Lord of Full Completion
Vanquished the army of the King of Destruction,
Tasted the ghee without compare, and attained
The supreme enlightenment of perfection.

King Aśoka offered a hundred thousand taels of gold to the Bodhi tree, and, after constructing a stupa at the spot, went away to other places.

Upagupta again spoke to the king, saying, "This is the place where the Buddha received from the Four Heavenly Kings four alms bowls, which he merged into one." He said at another place, "This is the place where the Buddha accepted food offered by the two merchants Trapuṣa and Bhallika. From here the Buddha went to the country of Vārāṇasī." There was also the place where the heretic named Upajeta praised the Tathāgata.

138a Upagupta also took King Aśoka to Mṛgadāva, the park of recluses, and pointed to it, saying, "This is the place where the World-honored One turned thrice the Wheel of the Dharma of the twelve *nidāna*s (links of causality)." And he also uttered the following stanza:

At this place he turned three times
The Wheel of the Dharma of the twelve *nidāna*s,
Created by the Dharma of truth,
To save all beings from the pains of rebirth.

This was the place where one thousand heretics became Buddhist monks.

There was another place where the Buddha preached the Dharma to King Biṃbisāra, who thereupon realized correct views. At another place the Buddha preached the Dharma to eighty thousand heavenly beings and numerous Brahmans and householders of the country of Magadha, who thereupon realized correct views. There was another place where the Buddha preached the Dharma to the heavenly king Śakra together with eighty thousand heavenly beings, who thereupon realized correct views. There was another place where the World-honored One returned to earth with numerous heavenly beings after having preached the Dharma to his mother and spent the summer retreat at her abode in heaven. There were many more places, as has been extensively recorded.

Upagupta then took King Aśoka to Kuśinagara, where the Buddha entered nirvana. He raised his hand to show the king, saying, "Your Majesty, this is the place where the Tathāgata entered complete nirvana after having done what ought to be done." And he also uttered the following stanza:

Heavenly beings and Asuras,
Yakṣas, Nāgas, and other deities,
And all beings in the world
Having been fully edified,
The great zealous one of compassion
Entered nirvana, the state of completion.

Upon hearing these words, King Aśoka fainted and fell to the ground. When cold water was sprinkled on his face, he recovered his senses and stood up from the ground. After offering a hundred thousand taels of gold to the place of the Tathāgata's nirvana for the construction of a stupa, he worshipped at the feet of Upagupta and said to him, "As it has been predicted by the World-honored One that I should be his great disciple, I intend to make offerings to his relics." Upagupta said in reply, "Excellent! Excellent! The king's mind is very good!"

Upagupta then took King Aśoka to the Jeta Grove and pointed to it with his right hand, saying, "Your Majesty, this is the stupa of Śāriputra, to which you should make offerings." King Aśoka inquired of Upagupta, "What were the merits and wisdom of Śāriputra?" Upagupta answered that Śāriputra, being second only to the Buddha, was a general of the Dharma who always followed the Tathāgata to turn the Wheel of the Dharma. He was the foremost in wisdom among all disciples of the Buddha. The wisdom of all people in the world, the Tathāgata excepted, was less than one-sixteenth of his wisdom. Then Upagupta uttered the following stanza:

The unequalled Wheel of the Right Dharma
Was turned for the world by the Buddha.
Śāriputra followed him to turn the Wheel
For the world's benefit.
Who can talk about this person
And about the sea of his wisdom and merit?

138b Greatly pleased, King Aśoka offered a hundred thousand taels of gold to the stupa of Śāriputra and uttered the following stanza with his hands joined palm to palm:

I worship Śāriputra
With a mind of veneration.
Great wisdom removes distress
And gives the world illumination.

Upagupta then showed King Aśoka the stupa of Maudgalyāyana and said, "Your Majesty, this is the stupa of Maudgalyāyana, to which you should make offerings." The king inquired what the merits and divine powers of this person were. The elder monk said in reply, "The Buddha said that he was the foremost in possessing supernatural powers among all his disciples. He could agitate with his toe the supreme Dharma hall of the heavenly king Śakra, and he could subdue the Nāga kings Nanda and Upananda." Then he uttered the following stanza:

> In divine powers Maudgalyāyana
> Was the foremost, as the Buddha said.
> He could shake with his toe
> The supreme hall of Śakra.
> Two Nāga kings he subdued,
> Nanda and Upananda.
> His merits and divine powers
> Were a sea that was fathomless.

King Aśoka offered a hundred thousand taels of gold to the stupa of Maudgalyāyana and uttered the following stanza with his hands joined palm to palm:

> Supreme divine powers
> Save one from the distress of rebirth.
> I am worshipping now
> The renowned Maudgalyāyana.

Upagupta pointed to another place and said, "This is the stupa of Mahākāśyapa, to which offerings should be made." King Aśoka inquired about the merits of this person, and the elder said in reply, "The Buddha said that he was the foremost in contentment with few desires and in the practice of eight kinds of asceticism. The Buddha once shared his seat with him and covered him with the Buddha's own robe. He converted suffering beings and upheld the Dharma-*piṭaka*." [Upagupta] also uttered the following stanza:

> The supreme field of great blessedness
> Practiced contentment with few desires
> And upheld the Buddha's Dharma-*piṭaka*

To save all suffering beings.
The Buddha shared his seat with him
And covered him with his robes.
Nobody could relate in full
The great sea of his merits.

King Aśoka again offered a hundred thousand taels of gold to the stupa of Mahākāśyapa and uttered the following stanza with his hands joined palm to palm:

He always stayed in caves,
In contentment, with few desires,
138c Free from distress and enmity,
Having gained the fruit of liberation.
For his power of peerless merits,
I pay him homage.

Upagupta then showed King Aśoka the stupa of Vakula and said, "Your Majesty, this is the stupa of Vakula, to which you should make offerings." King Aśoka inquired, "What were the merits of this person?" Upagupta replied, "Among the Buddha's disciples, he was foremost in keeping himself free from illness, but he never taught the Dharma to others even in one or two sentences." Then the king ordered his men to offer twenty cowries to the stupa. A minister asked King Aśoka, "Vakula was also an arhat like the others. Why did you offer only twenty cowries to his stupa, whereas you offered gold to the other stupas?" King Aśoka said, "You should listen to me."

The lamp of wisdom
Can dispel darkness.
Caring about one's own corporality
Does little benefit to the world.
Thus cowries I present
As an offering to this stupa.

At that moment, the twenty cowries moved from the stupa to the feet of King Aśoka. The minister was greatly surprised at the sight, and he said, "As this arhat had the mental power to live with few desires, he refused to accept alms even after his nirvana."

Upagupta then took King Aśoka to the stupa of Ānanda and said, "Your Majesty, this is the stupa of Ānanda, to which offerings should be made. He was the attendant disciple of the Tathāgata and could remember the Buddha's sayings. The Buddha said that among his disciples Ānanda was the foremost in hearing his sayings." Then he uttered the following stanza:

> This elder Ānanda,
> Honored by men and heavenly beings,
> Always keeping the Buddha's bowl,
> Possessed the mind of intelligence.
> He heard as much as the great sea;
> What he spoke were words of subtlety.
> Understanding the Buddha's meanings,
> Comprehending all the Dharma,
> Being the storehouse of merits,
> He was praised by the World-honored Buddha.

King Aśoka offered one crore of taels of gold to the stupa of Ānanda, and his minister asked him, "Why did you present the largest offering to this stupa?" King Aśoka replied, "Listen to me."

> The Dharmakāya (Body of Truth) of the World-honored
> Buddha
> Is pure without parallel.
> This he could accept and uphold.
> Thus I offer the best gift to him.
> 139a He lit the lamp of the Buddha's teaching
> To dispel the darkness of distress.
> By his power the Dharma is abiding;
> Thus I offer the best gift to him.
> As the water in an ox track
> Is not comparable to the great sea,
> The water of the wisdom of Ānanda
> Is not comparable to the sea of the Buddha's wisdom.
> In the Sutras the Buddha ascended the throne

Together with him.
That is why I offer the best gift to him today.

After having made the offerings, King Aśoka was greatly pleased. He worshipped at Upagupta's feet and uttered the following stanza:

In my present human life,
I did not lose the fruit of a good deed.
It is by the power of my previous merits
That I have become a king of sovereignty.
Through what was falsity,
I gained the Dharma of reality.
Relic-stupas of the World-honored One
Adorn this mundane world.
But in the practice of austerity
Nothing have I yet done.

After worshipping at Upagupta's feet, King Aśoka returned to his own country.

Chapter III

The Causes of Making Offerings to the Bodhi Tree

King Aśoka offered a hundred thousand taels of gold each to the place where the Buddha was born, the place where he attained enlightenment, the place where he turned the Wheel of the Dharma, and the place where he entered nirvana. In the Bodhi tree, however, he felt the most faith and joy, and he pondered that as this was the place where the World-honored One had attained supreme perfect enlightenment he should offer the best gems and jewels to the tree every day.

King Aśoka's first lady, Tiṣyarakṣitā by name, was angry about it. "If the great king loves me, why should he give all the best gems and jewels to the Bodhi tree?" She called in a *caṇḍālī* (outcaste) maid and said to her, "The Bodhi tree is what I hate. Can you destroy it for me?" The maid said in reply, "Yes, I can, but you must pay me in gold." The lady said, "Let it be so."

139b The *caṇḍālī* maid cursed the tree with incantations and bound it with a cord, and so the tree withered away gradually. Someone reported it to the king, saying, "The Bodhi tree is dying away gradually." And he uttered the following stanza:

> Under the Bodhi tree the Buddha sat,
> Becoming omniscient in the world
> And gaining the wisdom of all knowledge.
> But the tree is now dying.

Upon hearing these words, the king fainted and fell to the ground. He recovered himself after his ministers sprinkled water on him for a long while. Sobbing and shedding tears, he uttered the following stanza:

> When I see this king of trees,
> It is like seeing the Tathāgata.
> If it withers away,
> My life will also expire.

On seeing that the king was so anxious and worried, the lady said to him, "If I cannot revive the Bodhi tree, then I also cannot please Your Majesty." The king said in reply, "If you can revive the Bodhi tree, then you are not a woman. Why? Because this is the place where the Buddha attained supreme perfect enlightenment."

The lady called the *caṇḍālī* maid and said to her, "Can you restore the tree to grow as before?" The maid replied, "If the root of the Bodhi tree is not dead, I can rejuvenate the tree to grow again." Then the *caṇḍālī* maid unloosed the cord with which she had bound the tree and dug a ditch around it. Every day she poured milk into the ditch to irrigate the tree, and in a few days it gradually revived and became alive as it was before. The people reported it to the king, saying, "Your Majesty has done a great meritorious deed. The Bodhi tree is growing again." Upon hearing these words, the king was very happy, and he went to the Bodhi tree and gazed at it without blinking. Then he uttered the following stanza:

> Beginning from King Bimbisāra,
> To the kings of different times,
> None of them could perform
> These two supreme causes:
> To water this tree of enlightenment
> With milk of good color and fragrance.
> I also present gifts
> To the holy monks of the five sects.

King Aśoka filled a thousand golden, silver, and lapis lazuli bottles with scented water and carried different kinds of food, drink, and flowers to bathe the tree with the scented water contained in the

thousand bottles. He also draped the tree with silk draperies of different colors. At that time the king also observed the Eight Precepts. After receiving the Eight Precepts, he ascended the audience hall with a thurible in his hand and invited the monks of the four quarters, saying, "May all the disciples of the World-honored One in the four quarters come here to take me in to
139c the teachings of the Buddha!" And he also uttered the following stanza:

> The sons of the Sugata of right conduct,
> Whose sense organs are pure and free from desires,
> Worthy of worship and great fields of blessedness,
> Are refuges for men and Devas.
> The supreme sons of the Sugata
> Are free from desires and practice *dhyāna*;
> Upon them the Asuras rely;
> May they come to take me in.
> In the country of Kaśmīra,
> In the great and secluded woods,
> There live many arhats;
> May they come to take me in.
> The sons of the Tathāgata rejoicing in *dhyāna*
> Live at Lake Anavatapta,
> Beside rivers, and in caves on the hills;
> May they come with pity for me.
> The sons of the Tathāgata with good words
> Live in the halls of *śarīra*s (relics)
> With minds of compassion free from worries;
> May they come to take me in.
> Possessing divine powers of great bravery,
> Living on Mount Gandhamādana,
> Are the arhats I invite;
> May they all come to this site.

When King Aśoka had uttered this stanza, three hundred thousand *bhikṣu*s, of whom a hundred thousand were harmonious arhats and two hundred thousand were learners, and numerous zealous ordinary people, gathered together, but nobody among the Sangha took the chief seat. King Aśoka said to the Elder Yaśas, who possessed the six supernatural powers, "Why is it that nobody is sitting on the first seat?" The Elder replied, "Because it is the seat for the chief Elder." The king said again, "Is there anybody even higher than Your Reverence?" The Elder replied, "Yes. The Buddha said that among his disciples the foremost in preaching, like the roar of a lion, was the person surnamed Bhāradvāja and named Piṇḍola. The chief seat is for him."

Upon hearing these words, King Aśoka was so excited that his hair stood on end like *kadamba* flowers. He said, "Most Virtuous One, is there any *bhikṣu* who saw the Buddha before he entered nirvana and is still living now?" The Elder replied, "Yes, the person who is surnamed Bhāradvāja and named Piṇḍola saw the Buddha." The king then inquired, "But can I see him today?" The Elder said in reply, "You will see him in a moment; he is coming now." The king was greatly pleased to hear these words and uttered the following stanza:

A great benefit I shall gain,
And I shall be converted in a peerless way
By seeing one of great virtue;
Piṇḍola is his name.

King Aśoka put his hands palm to palm and looked at the air
140a without moving his eyes for a moment. Then Piṇḍola, followed by innumerable arhats surrounding him in a group shaped like a crescent moon, descended from the air like a king goose and sat on the first seat.

At that time, King Aśoka saw the arrival of Piṇḍola Bhāradvāja; and all the *bhikṣus* from the ten quarters stood up from their seats. He saw that Piṇḍola had silvery hair and that the skin of his forehead as well as his eyebrows were hanging down over his face in the manner of a *pratyekabuddha*. Upon seeing him the king prostrated himself, like a big tree falling to the ground, to worship Piṇḍola. He kissed the monk's feet, knelt before him with his hands joined palm to palm, and looked at him shedding tears, while he uttered the following stanza:

> The earth has the sea as its garment,
> With mountains as canopies for its adornment.
> Having done away with my foes,
> I, Aśoka, owned this earth,
> Which made me delighted with pleasure.
> Even more am I delighted today,
> To meet you, a great virtuous man.
> As I see you today,
> I feel doubly happy in my mind.

He also asked, "Did you, Reverend Sir, ever see the World-honored One?"

Piṇḍola parted his long eyebrows with both hands to look at King Aśoka and uttered the following stanza:

> I saw the Tathāgata several times,
> The peerless and unparalleled one
> Who possessed the thirty-two marks,
> Whose face was like the autumnal full moon,
> Whose pure voice dissolved affliction,
> Entering the *samādhi* of non-disputation.

King Aśoka inquired again, "Where and how did Your Reverence see the Buddha?" The Elder said in reply, "Your Majesty, the World-honored One stayed at first in the city of Rājagṛha with a following of five hundred passion-free arhats. As I was among the group, I had the opportunity to see him." Then he uttered the following stanza:

> The passion-free Mahāmuni
> Was followed by passion-free arhats.
> When they were staying there,
> I could see him by good chance.
> Just as you see me today,
> I saw the Buddha in the same way.

140b “Again, Your Majesty, the World-honored One, in order to subdue the heretics, once manifested in the country of Śrāvastī various supernatural powers and appeared as numerous metamorphosed Buddhas with dignified physical marks and signs, ascending one heaven after another up to the Akaniṣṭha heaven. I was also present on that occasion and witnessed the different divine transformations of the Buddha.” Then he uttered the following stanza:

There were many heretics,
Practicing different erroneous ways.
The World-honored One subdued them
With his supernormal powers.
I saw the Buddha at that time,
Giving the world happiness.

“Again, Your Majesty, after staying for the summer retreat in the Thirty-three heavens to preach the Dharma to his mother, the World-honored One, surrounded by heavenly beings, descended to the country of Sāṃkāśya. As I was then among the congregation, I saw the heavenly beings, and I saw the *bhikṣuṇī* named Utpalavarṇikā transforming herself into the form of a *cakravartin* king possessing all of the seven kinds of treasures.” He then uttered the following stanza:

After his rainy season retreat in Heaven,
The Buddha descended from there.
As I was among the congregation,
I had the chance to see the Buddha.

“Again, Your Majesty, once Sumāgadhā, daughter of Anāthapiṇḍada, invited the Buddha and five hundred arhats. The Buddha went by his divine power to the country of Puṇḍravardhana, while I, carrying a mountain, also went through the air to the country by divine power. On that occasion the Tathāgata instructed me, saying, ‘You must not enter nirvana so long as my Dharma abides in the world.’” Piṇḍola then uttered the following stanza:

At the invitation of Sumāgadhā,
The Buddha went there by divine power.

I followed him to the land of Puṇḍra,
Raising a mountain high by my own power.
The Buddha instructed me on that occasion
To live in the world so long as the Dharma abides.
That was the condition upon which
I was able to see the Buddha.

"Again, Your Majesty, when you were a child in a previous life, you offered sand with a childish mind to the Buddha, while I offered him cooked rice, when he entered the city of Rājagṛha to collect alms. Rādhagupta rejoiced at the event. The Buddha made a prediction, saying, 'A hundred years after my nirvana, this child will become a *cakravartin* king with the name of Aśoka, rule over one of the four continents, and be a Dharma King. He will construct eighty-four thousand Dharmarāja stupas for the enshrinement of relics.' I was then among the congregation." He then uttered the following stanza:

The king was then a child,
When with folded hands he offered sand.
I was there at that moment
And witnessed the event.

King Aśoka again inquired of Piṇḍola, "Where does Your Reverence live?" He replied with the following stanza:

North of Lake Anavatapta,
On the mountain Gandhamādana:
I live at that place
With my fellow monks.

King Aśoka again asked Piṇḍola, "How many people follow Your Reverence?" He replied with the following stanza:

140c Sixty thousand arhats
Follow and surround me.
I and my congregation
Are free from the bane of passion.

"Again, Your Majesty, why are you so inquisitive about these matters? You should now quickly offer food to the monks. When the monks have taken their meal, I will talk with you again." The king said in reply, "Yes, I shall do as you advise. In order to remember the Buddha, I should go to see the Bodhi tree. After seeing the Bodhi tree, I shall offer a meal of different kinds of food and drink to the monks."

King Aśoka said to a *bhikṣu* named Sarvamitra, "I am going to offer a hundred thousand taels of gold and a thousand golden, silver, and lapis lazuli water pots to the monks. Make an announcement in the assembly in my name that this offering is made to the monks of the five sects."

At that time King Aśoka's son Kuṇāla was by the right side of the king. As the prince was in fear of his father, he dared not speak but raised two fingers to show to the announcer *bhikṣu* that he would offer twice as many gifts as his father. Upon seeing that Kuṇāla was going to present twice as many gifts as his father, the whole assembly laughed merrily. When the king saw that the assembly was laughing, he said to his minister Rādhagupta, "You must have made some mistake that caused the people to laugh." Rādhagupta said in reply, "As more people are wishing to perform meritorious deeds, if Your Majesty wishes to do the same, it befits Your Majesty to offer twice as many gifts as were intended." King Aśoka said in reply, "I shall offer three hundred thousand taels of gold to the monks and fill three thousand precious water pots with scented water to irrigate the Bodhi tree. Make an announcement in my name that the gifts are offered to the monks of the five sects."

Kuṇāla then raised four fingers to show to the *bhikṣus*. Greatly enraged, the king said to the minister Rādhagupta, "Now I am performing meritorious deeds. Who is so ignorant of worldly decorum as to compete with me?" On seeing that the king was getting angry, Rādhagupta saluted him at his feet and told him who dared to compete with him in the performance of meritorious deeds by uttering the following stanza:

Who dares to compete with the king
In the act of merit making?

It is no one else but Kuṇāla
Who is competing with the monarch.

When Aśoka turned to his right he saw Prince Kuṇāla and said to Piṇḍola, "Most Virtuous One, with the exception of my treasure house in which are stored the seven kinds of precious things, I offer everything, including all my land, palace attendants, ministers, as well as myself and Kuṇāla, to the Sangha. Make an announcement in my name to the assembly that I offer everything to the monks of the five sects." And he also uttered the following stanza:

Everything in my palace,
Excepting my treasures,
But including attendants and courtiers,
I offer to the monks.
The monks of the congregation
Are fields of blessing.
I and my prince
Shall gain merits.

141a After having presented alms to Piṇḍola and all the monks in the assembly, King Aśoka constructed a wall around the Bodhi tree. He personally climbed up to the top of the wall and poured four thousand water pots of scented water to irrigate the tree, which started to grow as before. And he uttered the following stanza:

I shall irrigate the Bodhi tree,
Which is now growing again,
With rich boughs and foliage,
And more merits shall I gain.

Having been watered by the king, the Bodhi tree started to grow as before, with green and pliant branches and leaves, and it unfolded new buds, to the great delight of the king and his ministers and people. Food and drink were then offered to the monks.

In the assembly there was a monk of great virtue by the name of Yaśas, who said to the king, "This assembly of monks is truly to be adored and respected. You should make offerings to it without a mind of discrimination." King Aśoka served food to the monks with his own hands, from the highest in order to the last one. At the end of the order there were two novices who made joy buns out of cooked rice and threw them to each other for fun. King Aśoka was amused to see them and thought that the two novices were playing like children.

The king went again to serve the chief monk with food and gradually came to the presence of Yaśas, who said to him, "Your Majesty should not harbor any feeling of disbelief towards any monk in the assembly." The king consented, but he told the Elder Yaśas that two novices were having fun with cooked rice. Yaśas said in reply, "Those two novices are arhats, having gained freedom of mind and wisdom." The king was greatly delighted to hear this.

Then he thought in his mind, "Now that I have offered food to the monks, I should get some good robes to offer to the two novices." Having read the mind of the king, one of the novices produced by his power of merits an iron vessel and placed it before him, while the other one produced *gandha-jala* (fragrant water) and other things. When the king saw these things, he asked, "What is the use of these things?" They replied, "Since Your Majesty wishes to present us with separate gifts of robes after offering food to the monks, we intend to dye the new robes." Upon hearing these words, the king thought in his mind, "I was just thinking within my mind and did not say anything. How did these persons come to know my mind?" Then he prostrated himself on the ground to worship at the feet of the two novices and uttered the following stanza to them:

> I, king of the Maurya clan,
> And my courtiers and men
> Have done deeds of merit
> And gained great benefits.
> I have faith in zealousness
> And have given what I can in alms.

141b King Aśoka said to the two novices, "On your account, I shall offer three robes to each of the monks in the assembly." So, after having performed meritorious deeds for the monks of the five sects, King Aśoka also presented three robes to each of them, besides offering four hundred thousand taels of gold to them. He also paid a large amount of gold and silver to redeem his land, palace attendants, and ministers, as well as himself and Kuṇāla.

The Causes of Vītaśoka

King Aśoka had a mind of deep faith in the Buddha-dharma. After constructing eighty-four thousand stupas, he convened an assembly of monks of the five sects, to whom he offered food and drink. There were in the assembly three hundred thousand arhats, twice as many learners, and innumerable zealous ordinary people, in whom the king had double faith.

At that time, King Aśoka's younger brother, Vītaśoka, believed in the dharma of the heretics, and he said, "None of Śākyamuni's disciples has attained emancipation. Why? Because they always take delight in a pleasurable way of life and dread asceticism." King Aśoka said to his younger brother, "Do not fix your faith in the wrong place. You should believe in the Buddha-dharma."

At another time when King Aśoka went out hunting, his younger brother saw a hermit in the mountains who was scorching himself with heat from five directions while earnestly practicing asceticism. Vītaśoka went up to worship at his feet and said, "Most Virtuous One, how long have you been staying here?" The hermit said in reply, "Twelve years." The prince asked again, "What food do you eat?" The hermit answered, "I often eat the fruits and roots of trees." The prince again inquired, "What clothes do you wear?" The hermit replied, "I weave cogon grass to make myself a robe." "What about your bedding?" asked the prince. "I spread grass on the ground," answered the hermit. The prince asked again, "What makes you feel so distressed?" The hermit replied, "When I saw two deer mating, the sight aroused my lustful desire; and the fire of lustful desire is burning in my heart." Then Vītaśoka entertained a doubt in his mind and reflected, "Even this ascetic has lustful desire, so how could the disciples of the Buddha, always living a pleasurable life, be free from passion if they saw the same sight? If they have desire in their minds, how could they cherish the notion of detesting and forsaking desire?" And he uttered the following stanza:

> The hermit in the wood of mortification,
> Living upon fruits, roots, and flowers,
> Breathing air without taking foul nutrition,
> Cannot quell his carnal desire.
> Sons of Śākyamuni Buddha
> Eat milk foods and butter,
> Wear robes of many types,
> And never give up one piece.
> If they could keep their senses under control,
> Mount Vaiḍūrya would be able to float.

141c King Aśoka's younger brother also said that the Śākya disciples were cheating the king into performing meritorious deeds. Upon hearing these words, King Aśoka, trying to employ some expedient, said to his minister, "My younger brother believes in the heretics. We should try to employ some expedient to convert him to the Buddha-dharma." In reply to the king, the minister said, "What does Your Majesty wish me to do?" The king told him, "Now I am going to the bathroom to take a bath. I shall take off my crown and garments. You may dress my younger brother in my costume and ask him to ascend the throne." The minister said in reply, "Yes."

King Aśoka then went to the bathroom to take off his ornaments, and after the king had entered the bathroom, the minister said to his younger brother, "You would have been king if it had not been for Aśoka. Now you may try to put on this crown and the royal garments and ascend the throne." Having said so, the minister dressed the prince in the king's garments and caused him to ascend the throne.

The minister then reported to King Aśoka, saying, "Your servant has carried out the order of Your Majesty." King Aśoka came to see his younger brother, who was wearing the crown and sitting on the throne, and said to him, "So you have assumed kingship even when I am not dead!" In a fit of rage the king called in the executioner, a fellow dressed in dark blue with dishevelled hair and holding a bell in his hand. Having come into the presence of the king, the executioner paid homage to him and said, "What do you wish me to do?" The king said, "I have discarded this younger brother of mine. You may kill him." When the king had said this, a group of people holding weapons in their hands came up to surround the prince.

At that moment the minister saluted the king's feet and said to him, "This is Your Majesty's younger brother, and I beg Your Majesty to have patience and not to be angry with him." King Aśoka said to the minister in reply, "I shall be patient with him for seven days. As he is my younger brother, I shall give him the kingdom temporarily, allow him to be king for seven days, and provide him with various musicians and maids of honor for his amusement. All people should come to pay respects to him."

Standing at the gate with a knife in hand, the executioner announced to the king every day, "One day has passed. There will be six days more!" [and so on.] So on the sixth day, he announced that there remained only one more day. On the seventh day, the royal ornaments, crown, and garments were returned to King Aśoka. The minister and other people took Vītaśoka to see the king, who asked him, "During the seven days of your kingship, how did you enjoy the pleasant music and various kinds of amusement?" In reply, the king's brother uttered the following stanza:

He who has seen the beauties,
Heard the melodies,
And tasted the delicacies
May answer your inquiries.

The king said again, "I gave you the kingdom so that you were king for seven days, and you enjoyed all kinds of amusement to your
142a heart's content, while numerous people came every day to pay homage and express good wishes to you. How can you say that you

did not see, hear, or taste anything delightful?" In reply, the prince again uttered the following stanza:

In the last seven days
I neither saw nor heard anything,
Nor did I smell or taste flavor.
I could not feel the touch
Of the ornaments I was wearing,
Or of the charming maids who were attending.
As I was thinking of dreadful death,
I lost the sensations of these things.
The songs of the nautch girls dancing,
The palaces and bedding,
The land and all the treasures,
Aroused in me no pleasure.
I only saw the executioner
Standing at the gate with his cleaver.
I also heard the sound of his bell
That reminded me of the knell.
The nail of death reached my heart
And rendered me numb to the five pleasures.
Being ill with fear of departing,
I could not sleep with composure.
While I thought death was approaching,
The night elapsed without my knowing.

King Aśoka then said to his younger brother, "Vītaśoka, as you were thinking of the pains of death just for one day, you did not attach yourself to the five best pleasures that were provided for you. In the same way, the homeless *bhikṣus* meditate on the impermanence of the countless births and deaths on the basis of the twelve entrances. How can they have any passions? They also meditate on the pains of the hells and of the animals cruelly killing one another, on the hungry ghosts suffering from hunger and thirst, and on men always rushing about without ease to all places for a living, and also on the pains of the heavenly beings at the stage of decadence. All beings in these five ways of existence are suffering mentally and physically without happiness. The *bhikṣus* also consider that all the five *skandhas* are impermanent, painful, void, egoless, and unsubstantial, just like an empty village without inhabitants. As the five *skandhas* are void and without an ego, the world is burning with the fire of impermanence. Since the Buddha's disciples always contemplate in this way, how can they have any passions?" And he also uttered the following stanza:

Just for a single day
You pondered on the fear of death
Without joy and pleasure
Nor with a mind of attachment.
The disciples of the Buddha
Contemplate birth and death every day.
How can they have joy and pleasure
And harbor minds of delusion?
On their food and garments,
As well as on their bedding,
They meditate upon how to gain liberation,
Free from mental attachment.
142b They see the corporeal body as an enemy,
The three realms as a house on fire.
They think of expedients
By which to gain emancipation.
Taking deep delight in the law of liberation,
They crave none of the five desires.
Their minds resemble lotus flowers
Standing in water without getting wet.

King Aśoka employed this good expedient to convert Vītaśoka to the Buddha-dharma, and Vītaśoka, with folded hands, said to the king, "Your Majesty, I now take refuge in the Tathāgata as well as his Dharma and the Sangha." And he also uttered the following stanza:

I take refuge in the Buddha,
Whose face resembles a lotus flower,

A shelter for divine and human beings.
I also submit to the pure Dharma and the Sangha.

King Aśoka then embraced his younger brother's neck and said to him, "I do not discard you. It was for the sake of converting you to the Buddha-dharma that I adopted this expedient."

Vītaśoka offered various kinds of flowers and incense with the performance of music to the Buddha-stupas, and he also presented different kinds of food and drink as alms to the monks. Then he went to Kukkuṭa Monastery, where the Elder Yaśas, an arhat possessing the six supernatural powers, was residing. Upon arriving at the monastery, he sat face to face with Yaśas, wishing to hear the Dharma from him. With his supernormal powers, Yaśas perceived that Vītaśoka had done good deeds in his previous lives and that this was his last birth with a corporeal body, as he would attain arhatship. The Elder preached the Dharma and praised the renunciation of home life. After hearing the Dharma, Vītaśoka wished to renounce his home life and said to Yaśas with folded hands, "You have preached the Dharma and Vinaya (disciplinary rules) well. May I renounce my home to be a fully ordained monk? I wish to lead a life of celibacy according to the Buddha-dharma." Yaśas said in reply, "Good man, you may go back to ask King Aśoka whether he permits you to renounce your home." Vītaśoka returned to King Aśoka and said to him with folded hands, "May Your Majesty allow me to renounce the home life, as I wish to lead a life of celibacy according to the Buddha-dharma." And he also uttered the following stanza:

My mind is confused in distraction,
Like an unhooked elephant.
The king's will is an iron hook.
Do not stop me from leaving home.
The king is the lord of the earth,
And should allow me to leave my hearth.
For this world the Buddha is a ray,
And I wish to go along his Way.

Upon hearing these words, King Aśoka embraced his younger brother's neck and said with tears and sobbing, "Vītaśoka, do not conceive such an idea. Why? Because the monks wear coarse and shabby clothes, eat what is given by others, and sleep under trees.
142c Now stop thinking about becoming a monk." Vītaśoka said in reply, "Your Majesty, I wish to become a monk not out of hatred, or craving, or poverty, or to evade some enemy. It is simply because I see that this world is full of pain and continual rebirths without emancipation, and I see that the Buddha-dharma is the only right path leading to freedom from rebirth without fear. So I wish to become a monk with pleasure." King Aśoka sobbed more piteously when he heard these words. Vītaśoka then uttered the following stanza:

> Rebirth is like a rope hanging,
> Man is on it always swinging.
> What is on it will drop down.
> From union separation comes.

King Aśoka then said to his younger brother, "Before becoming a monk, you have to practice begging for alms." In the royal garden at the back of the palace, there was a big tree, under which grass was spread on the ground to provide a place for Vītaśoka to stay. An earthen bowl was given to him so that he could beg alms from the palace. With begging bowl in hand, he went to the palace, where he obtained different varieties of the choicest food. The king became angry with the palace attendants and said to them, "Why do you give the best food to the mendicant? From now on you should give him coarse food." Thus wheat was cooked and kept for a night and then given to him when it had turned sour. Vītaśoka accepted the food and ate it without feeling disgusted. At this sight, King Aśoka said to him, "Stop taking this food. I permit you to become a monk; but after becoming a monk, you should often come to see me."

Then Vītaśoka went to the Kukkuṭa Monastery, and when he reached there, he thought that if he became a monk at that place the people and environment would distract his mind from cultivating the Way, and that he should go to become a monk at some distant place. So he travelled to the country of Videha, where he became a monk and engaged himself in meditation vigorously until he attained arhatship.

Having attained arhatship, the Elder Vītaśoka enjoyed the bliss of emancipation and thought that as he had made an agreement with the king to see him often after becoming a monk, he should fulfill his promise.

Then he travelled by easy stages to the country of Pāṭaliputra. Early in the morning, the Elder Vītaśoka dressed himself and went to the city with his begging bowl to collect alms. He went from house to house and then to the palace of King Aśoka, where he said to the gatekeeper, "Go in and inform the king that Vītaśoka is outside the gate, wishing to see His Majesty." The gatekeeper went in and informed the king, saying, "Vītaśoka has arrived and wishes to see Your Majesty." King Aśoka said to the gatekeeper, "You may bring him into the palace." Vītaśoka then entered the palace, and upon seeing him, King Aśoka rose from his throne and
143a prostrated himself, like a great tree falling on the ground, in order to worship him. Then he stood up and gazed at him with his hands joined palm to palm without feeling weariness. He uttered the following stanza with tears of emotion:

> All living beings are happy
> To live in a harmonious family.
> But you renounced your home
> To live a life quiet and calm.
> Now I understand your mind.
> With no amount of wisdom are you content.

At that time, the minister Sugupta saw that Vītaśoka wore a robe made of cast-off rags. He carried an earthen bowl, went from house to house to collect alms, and without distinguishing in his mind accepted whatever food, coarse or fine, was given him. He said to King Aśoka, "Vītaśoka is content, with few desires, and has accomplished what he aimed to achieve. Your Majesty ought to be happy about it." Why?

He, always practicing alms-begging,
Wearing cast-off rag clothing,
Living beneath a tree,
Has a mind in constant *samādhi*.
His mind is broad without leakage;
His body is free from malady;
Leading a righteous life,
He is always cheerful.

King Aśoka was greatly pleased to hear these words, and he uttered the following stanza:

You abandoned the Maurya clan,
The kingdom of Magadha,
Precious jewels of every kind,
And the best enjoyment of the five desires.
You rejoice at the four noble truths,
Free from arrogance, pride, and distress,
Practicing the Way with great diligence.
My country is glorified by your eminence.
The supreme Dharma, the ten powers
You are qualified to possess.

King Aśoka helped him to the seat of honor and served different kinds of food and drink to him with his own hands. After the meal, his eating bowl was washed and put aside. King Aśoka sat before him to listen to his preaching, and in the course of preaching, Vītaśoka uttered the following stanza:

Mental freedom you have now gained;
Non-laxity should also be attained.
The Three Treasures are not easy to meet.
Offerings should often be made to them.

King Aśoka and five hundred courtiers, together with the people of the country, surrounded Vītaśoka respectfully with folded hands to send him off. The courtiers and people uttered the following stanza:

King Aśoka, the elder brother,
Sends off the younger one with respect.
The supreme fruit of renunciation
Is now fully realized.

In order to reveal his merits, the Elder Vītaśoka soared into the
143b air, and all the people saw his departure. King Aśoka and the multitude, folding their hands palm to palm, witnessed the event with fixed gaze, and [Aśoka] uttered the following stanza:

Without fraternal affection,
Like a bird you fly through the air.
I am bound by love and passion,
Unable to go as freely as I care.
The supreme fruit of meditation
Gives freedom to the body.
You may go anywhere at your discretion,
Without any impediment whatsoever.
Being blinded by lust and desire,
I could not see the Dharma.
By your supernormal powers,
You lifted me from lustful desire.
I was proud of my wisdom,
But you are the wisest of all.
We are attached to the world,
Not fearing it until we see the saint.
We are weeping and shedding tears,
Because you are leaving us forever.

Then the Elder Vītaśoka repaired to a borderland, and upon reaching there he fell so seriously ill that his head was covered with boils. The king, hearing about it, dispatched attendants and physicians to cure him. When he was a little better some time later, both the physicians and the attendants were sent back. As he needed only milk for his nourishment, he went for convenience of begging alms to live at a place where there were many cows.

There was then a country called Puṇyavardhana, where all the people believed in heretics. One man who followed the heretical dharma worshipped a naked god painted in the shape of the Tathāgata and paid homage to it at its feet. A Buddhist disciple saw this matter and reported it to King Aśoka. After hearing it, the king ordered that the man be brought into his presence. Now within the domain of King Aśoka, all the Yakṣas (demons) in the air up to the height of half a *yojana* were under his control, and all the Nāgas one *yojana* below the earth also belonged to him. Upon hearing the order of the king, the Yakṣas in an instant brought the heretical disciple and his picture into the presence of the king. Being greatly enraged by the sight, he had all the heretics of Puṇyavardhana killed; and one hundred eight thousand heretics were slaughtered in one day.

There was another heretical follower who accepted a heretical dharma, worshipped a naked god painted in the shape of the Tathāgata, and paid it homage at its feet. When King Aśoka heard about it, he again ordered his men to arrest that man and his relations, all of whom were put in a house, which was then set on fire. The king also issued a decree, saying, "If anyone can get the head of a Nirgrantha, I shall award him a piece of gold."

At that time, the Elder Vītaśoka came to a place where cows
143c were reared and spent one day there. As he had been sick for many days, his hair and beard were long, his nails were sharp, and he was wearing a coarse garment without color or brilliance. A cowherd woman thought in her mind, "Here comes a Nirgrantha to our house." And then she said to her husband, "You can kill this Nirgrantha and send his head to King Aśoka, and you will surely get a gold coin." The husband, hearing this, unsheathed his sword and went to Vītaśoka with the intention of decapitating him. The elder, reflecting that nowhere could one escape from one's retribution, faced death as it befell him. His head was then sent to King Aśoka by the man wishing to win the reward of gold.

When the king saw that the hair on the head was of an attractive variegated color, he had a suspicion in his mind and inquired of the physicians and attendants about it. They said to the king, "This is the head of Vītaśoka!" Upon hearing these words, the king fainted and fell to the ground. When water was sprinkled on him, he recovered and got to his feet after a long while.

A minister said to the king, "Even a man who is perfectly free from passions is not spared from this suffering. It befits Your Majesty to grant freedom from fear to living beings." Aśoka followed this advice and issued an order that no Nirgranthas should be killed any more.

Then the *bhikṣus* had a doubt about it and inquired of Upagupta, "What deed did Vītaśoka commit in the past, that he suffered this retribution of being murdered by another?"

Upagupta said in reply, "Elders, listen. In the past there was a hunter who killed many herds of deer. In the great forest there was a spring where the hunter spread his net and tied the rope beside the water. In this way he killed many deer every day. That was a time when the Buddha was not yet born in the world. One day a *pratyekabuddha* took his meal beside the water. After taking his meal, he bathed and went to sit underneath a tree. All the deer, smelling the fragrance of the *pratyekabuddha*, did not go to the waterside. When the hunter came and did not see any deer, he traced the footmarks and came to the *pratyekabuddha*. On seeing him, the hunter thought in his mind, 'It is because of this man sitting here that the deer did not come.' Thereupon he killed the *pratyekabuddha* with a knife. You should know, Elders, that that hunter of bygone days was today's Vītaśoka. As he had killed many deer every day in the past, he suffered various ailments in his present life. His murder of the *pratyekabuddha* caused him to suffer pains of every description in hells for innumerable years. He was always killed each of the five hundred times he was born as a human being. This was his last birth; but even though he had attained arhatship, he was still murdered by a man."

The *bhikṣus* again asked Upagupta, "But how did this person come to be born into a great clan and attain arhatship?" Upagupta said in reply, "Formerly, when he became a monk in the Dharma
144a of Kāśyapa Buddha, he loved to give alms and often advised lay supporters to offer various kinds of food and drink to the Sangha. There was then a stupa containing the Buddha's hair and nail

relics, to which he offered incense, flowers, banners, and canopies, as well as different kinds of musical performances. It was because of this karma that he was born into a great clan. And for a hundred thousand years he constantly practiced celibacy with a right vow, on account of which he attained arhatship."

Chapter IV

The Causes of Kuṇāla

King Aśoka constructed eighty-four thousand stupas in one day, and on that day his wife Padmāvatī gave birth to a son with regular features and particularly beautiful eyes. No one saw him but loved him. A palace attendant reported to the king that by the merits of the king, his wife had given birth to a son. The king was pleased to hear this news and uttered the following stanza:

I am today
Greatly pleased.
My clan of Maurya
Is well known to all.
May my son in the palace
Increase the Dharma!

Thus the child was named Dharmavivardhana (Dharma-increasing). Then he was carried in to be shown to the king, who was glad to see him and uttered the following stanza:

Beautiful are the eyes of my son,
Created by merits previously done.
Bright and very brilliant,
Resembling *utpala* (blue lotus) flowers,
These eyes of merit
Adorn his features.
His face is regular and dignified,
Like a full moon in the season of autumn.

King Aśoka assembled his ministers and said to them, "Have you ever seen eyes such as those of this child?" The ministers said in reply, "We have really never seen such eyes among human beings. But in the Snow Mountains there is a kind of bird called a *kuṇāla* whose eyes resemble the eyes of this child." And they uttered the following stanza:

On top of the Snow Mountains,
At the place of precious flowers,
The birds called *kuṇāla*
144b Stay in their nests.
The eyes of this child
Resemble those of the bird.

The king then ordered, "Bring that bird here." The Yakṣas in the air up to the height of half a *yojana* heard the king's words, and the Nāgas one *yojana* below also heard his words. In an instant, the Yakṣas brought a bird to the king, who compared its eyes with the eyes of his son and found no difference between them. Thus he gave the child the name of the bird and uttered the following stanza:

The king of men on the earth
Uses the name of *kuṇāla*,
With most beautiful eyes,
As his son's name,
So that on this earth,
His fame will spread far.

When Kuṇāla had grown up, he was given a lady named Kāñcanamālā to be his wife. Once King Aśoka brought him to Kukkuṭa Monastery, where lived an elderly monk by the name of Yaśas, an arhat possessing the six supernatural powers. At that moment Yaśas foresaw that before long Kuṇāla would lose his eyes. So he said to the king, "Why do you not ask Kuṇāla to do his own deeds?" King Aśoka said to Kuṇāla, "The Most Virtuous One asks you to do what you should do. You should follow him." Then Kuṇāla worshipped at Yaśas' feet and said to him, "Most Virtuous One, teach me what I should do." Yaśas said in reply, "Eyes are impermanent. You should meditate on this." And he also uttered the following stanza:

You, Kuṇāla,
Should meditate on the eyes
As impermanent with the pain of illness,
Where all things converge.
Ordinary people have upside-down views,
Giving rise to what is wrong.

Kuṇāla then sat alone at a quiet place in the palace to meditate that the eyes and other sense organs were painful and impermanent. King Aśoka's chief wife Tiṣyarakṣitā went to Kuṇāla and saw that he was sitting alone. When she saw his eyes, a surge of lustful desire arose in her mind and she embraced him with her arms while she uttered the following stanza:

A strong fire of love
Is burning in my heart,
Like flames licking a dry vine.
Come, you, to satisfy my mind.

When Kuṇāla heard these words of hers, he plugged his ears with his hands and uttered the following stanza:

At this place of mine,
No such words should be said.
You are a mother to me,
And I am a son to you.
Passions of this illegal kind
Should be put far away.
Why should you for this matter
Open the gate to the evil way?

144c As Tiṣyarakṣitā's desire was not satisfied, she became angry and resentful and uttered the following stanza:

I fixed my mind of love upon you,
But you have no love in your mind.
Since you dislike me,
You will soon be wiped out.

Kuṇāla said in reply:

I would rather die
For the Dharma of purity than live.
I would not stay in life
With a mind of obscenity.
One who has an evil mind
Loses the good Dharma of Devas and men.
If the good Dharma becomes imperfect,
On what will one's life depend?

Tiṣyarakṣitā kept a constant watch over him with the intention of killing him. There was then in the north a country named Takṣaśilā, which rebelled against King Aśoka's orders. When the king heard about it, he intended to go there himself, but his ministers said to him, "Kuṇāla should be ordered to go. There is no need for you to go yourself." King Aśoka summoned Kuṇāla and said to him, "You should go to that country." Kuṇāla replied to the king, "So be it." King Aśoka also uttered the following stanza:

At this moment,
I heard him saying, "So be it."
Though he is my son,
He is also my heart.
As I remember him in my mind,
He is more lovely to me.

King Aśoka then had the roads repaired. All corpses were removed and all aged and sick people were ordered to keep out of sight. The king rode in the same carriage with Kuṇāla to see him off. When they were about to part near the road, he embraced his son's neck and shed tears on seeing Kuṇāla's lovely eyes, while he said:

If anyone sees
Kuṇāla's lovely eyes
And is pleased,
All his ailments will be eased.

At that time, a Brahman physiognomist foresaw that Kuṇāla would soon lose his eyes. On seeing that the king was gazing at his son's eyes without paying attention to anything else, he uttered the following stanza:

> The prince has eyes of purity;
> When the king sees them he feels happy.
> Bright and beautiful are his eyes.
> Why should they be lost?
> All the people in this country,
> When they see Kuṇāla's eyes,
> Feel pleased,
> As if enjoying heavenly bliss.
> If they see him lose his eyes,
> They will all be distressed.

145a Kuṇāla then gradually proceeded to the country of Takṣaśilā. The people of that country, hearing about it, went out half a *yojana* to repair and decorate the road. They placed water everywhere in anticipation of the coming multitude. The people uttered the following stanza:

> The people of Takṣaśilā
> Hold water in precious jars
> And other offerings
> To greet Prince Kuṇāla.

When the prince arrived, the people folded their hands and said to him, "We do not come to meet you to fight, nor do we bear any grudge against the great king. But the minister sent by the king to our country governs the state unjustly, and we wish him to be dismissed from office." Then the people presented offerings to Prince Kuṇāla and welcomed him to their country.

King Aśoka then fell seriously ill; he vomited out of his mouth, and filthy fluid oozed from his pores. All the best physicians failed to cure him. King Aśoka said to his ministers, "Recall Kuṇāla. I shall consecrate him king and hand over the throne to him. Now I shall cling to this life no more."

Tiṣyarakṣitā thought in her mind, "If Kuṇāla becomes king, I shall certainly be put to death." With this reflection in her mind, she said to King Aśoka, "I can cure the king and get rid of the disease. There is no need to send for any more physicians." So the king listened to her words and refused to see any physicians. Tiṣyarakṣitā said to the physicians, "If there is anybody outside, male or female, who is suffering from the same disease as the king, you may bring that person in."

There was then in the country of the Ābhīras a man suffering from the same trouble as the king. The sick man's wife consulted a physician and told him the symptoms of her husband's illness. The physician said in reply, "Bring the man here. I wish to see him and write out a prescription for him." Thus the woman brought the patient to the physician, who then sent him to the king's wife.

The king's wife put the sick man in a secluded place, had his abdomen cut open, and extracted both his "raw" and his "ripe" viscera. In his ripe viscus there was a big worm, and when it moved upwards vomit was ejected out of the mouth. Excrement was discharged below when it moved downwards. If it moved sideways, filthy fluids oozed from the pores. The king's wife ground some *mallikā* (jasmine) and placed it beside the worm, but it did not die. She then put some *pippalī* (long pepper) beside it, and it still did not die. She again placed some dry ginger near the worm, and it still did not die. But it died instantly when she placed some garlic beside it.

The king's wife reported this matter to the king, saying, "The king should now eat some garlic, which will cure the disease."
145b The king said in reply, "Being a Kṣatriya, I should not eat garlic." The lady said, "For the sake of your body and life, it should be taken as medicine." So King Aśoka ate some garlic, and the worm was then killed and his disease was cured. Thus he became as fit and lively as before.

After having bathed, King Aśoka said to his wife, "Whatever you desire to have now, I shall grant you as you wish." The king's wife said to him, "May the king allow me to be king for seven days." The king said to his wife, "If you become king, you will certainly kill me." His wife said again, "After seven days, I shall return the kingship to you." Thus King Aśoka granted her the request.

The king's wife reflected, "This is now the right time for me to punish Kuṇāla." Then she wrote a false letter in the name of King Aśoka to the people of Takṣaśilā, asking them to gouge out Kuṇāla's eyes. In the letter, there was written the following stanza:

I am now very powerful,
My prestigious name, fearful.
As Kuṇāla, the prince,
Has committed an offence,
Now I order you people
To extract his two eyes.
To perform this matter now
You should take action in haste.

When the royal lady had written this letter, she needed to impress it with the king's dental marks. King Aśoka was then sleeping, and as the lady wished to seal the letter she went close to the king. The king woke up with a start. The lady asked the king, "Why are you frightened and startled?" The king said in reply to the lady, "I had an inauspicious dream in which I saw a vulture attempting to extract Kuṇāla's eyes. This is why I was startled with fear." The lady said in reply, "The king need not be worried. Prince Kuṇāla is now quite safe and sound." In the second watch, the king had another dream; and he was again wakened from sleep with a start. He said to the lady, "I had another dream as ominous as the first one." The lady asked, "What was it?" The king said in reply, "I saw that Kuṇāla had long hair, a beard, and sharp nails; and he was unable to speak." The lady said, "He is safe and sound. Do not worry about him."

Afterwards when King Aśoka fell asleep, the lady stealthily had the letter impressed with the king's teeth and had it sent to the people of Takṣaśilā.

At that time, King Aśoka again dreamed that all his teeth had fallen out. When he had taken a bath early the next morning, he summoned as a life-and-death matter a physiognomist and told him everything he had seen in his dream, saying, "You should read the meaning of my dream." The physiognomist said in reply, "If anyone has had such a dream, his son will lose his sight. That is just like losing one's son." Then he uttered the following stanza:

> If anyone dreams that his teeth have fallen out,
> His son will lose his sight.
> Since one's son has lost his eyes,
> It is the same as losing one's son.

145c When King Aśoka heard these words, he stood up facing the deities of the four quarters with folded hands and implored their protection with vows, saying:

> I take refuge single-heartedly in the Buddha,
> In the pure Dharma, and in the Sangha.
> All the recluses of this earth
> Are most eminent in the world.
> May all saintly monks
> Extend protection to Kuṇāla.

When the messenger arrived with the letter in the country of Takṣaśilā, the people of the country, upon seeing the letter, hid it away and did not give it to Kuṇāla. They had affection for him and did not wish to cause resentment in his mind. The people also reflected, "Since the great King Aśoka is so fearful that he has neither esteem nor confidence even in his own son and wishes to extract his eyes, how can he treat us without malignance?" And they uttered the following stanza:

> Now as regards this Kuṇāla,
> He is no different from a great recluse.
> Of all living beings
> He is the benefactor.
> But to him the great king Aśoka
> Has no mind of compassion,

Let alone to any other beings.
He will spare none from cruelties.

At last the people gave the letter to Kuṇāla. Upon receiving the letter, Kuṇāla said to the people, "If anyone can extract my eyes, he may do so at his own discretion." The people then called in a *caṇḍāla* and said to him, "Extract Kuṇāla's eyes." The *caṇḍāla* said with folded hands, "I cannot do that. Why?"

If a man could erase
The full moon's brilliant light,
He might extract the eyes
From your face, a moon that is bright.

Kuṇāla took off his precious coronet and said to the *caṇḍāla*, "If you can extract my eyes, I shall give this to you." There was another man of abominable features marked with the eighteen marks of ugliness, who said, "I can extract your eyes."

At that moment Kuṇāla remembered what the most virtuous Yaśas had told him, and he uttered the following stanza:

Things united must be separated:
This is a true saying.
When I think of this teaching,
I know that my eyes are not abiding.
My good teacher of the Way
Is able to benefit me.
What he preaches on the Dharma
Concerns the causes and conditions of suffering.
I always remember and ponder
That everything is impermanent.
This was taught by my teacher,
And I should deeply keep it in mind.
I do not fear the pain,
As I have seen that nothing is everlasting.
In compliance with the king's order,
146a You may extract my eyes.

I have already imbibed
The truth of impermanence.

Kuṇāla then said to the ugly man, "You may gouge out one of my eyes and place it in my palm, as I wish to see it." When that ugly man was about to take out Kuṇāla's eye, numerous people angrily scolded him and uttered the following stanza:

His eyes are pure and without stain,
Like the moon in the air.
You are extracting his eyes,
As one might pull a lotus from a pond.

Numerous people wailed and wept piteously, while the ugly man took out Kuṇāla's eye and put it in his hand. Accepting his eye in his hand, Kuṇāla uttered the following stanza to it:

Originally, in former times,
You could see all colors.
But at this moment now,
Why can you not see them?
Formerly you caused the seer
To have a mind of attachment;
Now I see that you are not real,
But false and unsubstantial
Like a bubble on water
That is void and without entity.
You are simply powerless
And not independent.
One who sees this point
Will suffer no more pains.

When Kuṇāla was meditating on the impermanence of all dharmas, he attained the fruition of a *srota-āpanna*. After having gained the fruit, he said to the ugly man, "You may gouge out my other eye as you like." The ugly man then cut out the other eye and placed it in Kuṇāla's hand. Although he had lost his eyes of flesh, he obtained the Eye of Wisdom; and then he uttered the following stanza:

At this moment now,
I forsake my eyes of flesh.
The Eye of Wisdom is hard to gain,
But I have gained it now.
The king has abandoned me;
I am no more the king's son.
As I have gained the Dharma,
I am a son of the Dharma King.
Now I have freely fallen
From the palace of suffering,
And also freely ascended
To the palace of the Dharma King.

Knowing that it was Tiṣyarakṣitā who wanted to extract his eyes, Kuṇāla uttered the following stanza:

May the king's spouse
Always enjoy wealth and bliss.
May she live forever
And never come to an end.
It was through her expedient that
My aim has been gained.

When Kuṇāla's wife Kāñcanamālā heard that Kuṇāla had lost his eyes, she went to her husband out of anxiety about him. At a place where there was a crowd of people, she saw Kuṇāla, who had lost his eyes and was bleeding. Thus she fainted and fell to the ground, and people sprinkled water on her to restore her to consciousness. She wept and uttered the following stanza:

146b Your eyes were bright and lovable;
When I saw them formerly they were pleasurable.
Now they are apart from your body;
They cause in my mind a great worry.

Kuṇāla said to his wife, "Do not weep. As I have done the deeds, I am receiving the retribution." He also uttered the following stanza:

Everyone in this world
Receives his body according to his deeds.
The body is formed by pains of diverse kinds;
This you should understand.
All sorts of unions
Are bound to end in separation.
This matter you should know.
There is no need to weep with lamentation.

Kuṇāla and his wife then returned to King Aśoka's palace from the country of Takṣaśilā. As the two of them had never before, since their birth, walked on the ground, they were so weak and feeble that they could not bear the hardship of their labor. Kuṇāla was good at playing the lute as well as singing and playing wind instruments. They followed the original road and begged for food to sustain their lives. Gradually they reached their own country and intended to enter the palace gate, but the gatekeeper did not allow them to go in. Since they could not get in, they withdrew and lodged in a carriage shed and stable. In the third division of the night, Kuṇāla played his lute and started singing a song with the words, "My eyes are lost, but the four noble truths have I seen." And he also sang the following song:

If a man possessing wisdom
Sees the twelve entrances
With the lamp of wisdom,
He may be free from rebirth.
The sufferings of the three realms of being
Are the sufferings of one's own mind.
As for all faults of the three realms of being,
One should perceive them now.
If one wishes to acquire supreme bliss,
One should ponder on the twelve entrances.

When King Aśoka heard the voice singing the song, he was greatly pleased and uttered the following stanza:

Now the song that is being sung
And the sound of the lute
Sound like my son.
Kuṇāla's voice is heard;
If he has arrived,
Why does he not come to see me?

King Aśoka called in a man [and said], "The voice I heard seemed to be that of Kuṇāla; it was so melodious and yet so sad and sorrowful. That voice distracted my mind, as an elephant is restless with an uneasy mind when it has lost its son but hears its son's trumpeting. You may go to see whether it is Kuṇāla or not. If it is Kuṇāla, then bring him here."

Under the king's order, that man went to the carriage shed and stable, where he saw a man who had lost both eyes and whose skin was tanned by the sun; he did not recognize the prince. He went back to report to the king, saying, "The person Your Majesty ordered me to see is a lonely blind man, staying with his wife in the carriage shed and stable. He is not Kuṇāla." Upon hearing
146c these words, King Aśoka felt distressed and pondered over the matter. And then he uttered the following stanza:

I saw in a dream before
That Kuṇāla had lost his eyes.
Now this blind man
Must be Kuṇāla without doubt.
Go there again
To bring him to this place.
As I am thinking of my son,
My mind is not at ease.

The man went again to the shed and asked Kuṇāla, "Whose son are you? What is your name?" Kuṇāla replied with the following stanza:

My father is named Aśoka-vardhana,
With the surname of Maurya.
The whole great earth

Is under his control,
And I am his prince,
By the name of Kuṇāla,
Surnamed Dharmarāja Buddha.
I am the son of the Dharma King.

The messenger then brought Kuṇāla and his wife to the palace. King Aśoka saw that Kuṇāla had been exposed to wind and sunburned and was dressed in a garment made of grass and rags, and that his appearance had changed beyond recognition. With a doubt arising in his mind, King Aśoka asked him, "Are you Kuṇāla?" "Yes, I am," was the reply. When King Aśoka heard this, he fainted and fell to the ground. An attendant saw what had happened to the king and uttered the following stanza:

When the king saw that Kuṇāla
Had no eyes in his face,
A painful feeling burned in his heart.
He fell down from his sofa.

The attendant then sprinkled water on the king to make him recover his consciousness. The king then returned to his seat and carried Kuṇāla and sat him on his lap, weeping and shedding tears and stroking his head and face, while he recollected his features of bygone days. And he uttered the following stanza:

Those handsome eyes of yours,
Where are they now?
The causes of losing your eyes
You should tell me.
Now you are deprived of your eyes,
As if the moon disappeared from the skies.
Your countenance has been altered.
By whom was it committed?
Your features in former days
Resembled those of the fairies.
Who is the one so merciless
As to have destroyed your eyes?

In this world of humanity,
Who has been your foe?
This is the root of my misery
That arose therefrom.
By whom was this graceful
Countenance of yours deformed?
The flames of mental fury
Are consuming my body.
It is like the thunder
That destroys a forest of trees.
The lightning of hatred
Has broken my heart.
147a The causes of such happenings
You should tell me without delay.

Kuṇāla answered with the following stanza:

Has not the king heard the Buddha's saying:
Retribution can never be avoided?
Even a *pratyekabuddha*
Is not to be exempted.
All worldly beings
Were created by their own karma.
All karmic deeds, good or bad,
Will produce their effects at the right times.
All sentient beings
Receive the result of what they have done.
As I understand the cause,
I do not blame the defacer of my eyes.
This suffering is caused by myself
And is not made by any other person.
Just like the karmic condition of my eyes,
Which was not made by any other person,
The sufferings of all living beings
Are created in the same way,
By their own karmic force.
The king should know such is the case.

King Aśoka, with a fire of resentment burning in his heart, again uttered the following stanza:

> You just tell me who it was
> And I shall not bear a mind of malice.
> If you do not make a clean breast of it,
> I shall feel distracted and disturbed.

When King Aśoka came to know that it was done by Tiṣyarakṣitā, he called in the lady and uttered the following stanza:

> Having committed an atrocity,
> Why do you not sink into the ground?
> You did not perform what was right
> But committed a great misdeed.
> Since you have done evil,
> I abandon you forever,
> Just as a good-deed performer
> Would give up filthy lucre.

When King Aśoka, with a fire of hatred burning in his heart, saw Tiṣyarakṣitā, he again uttered the following stanza:

> At this moment now
> I wish to extract her eyes
> And use an iron saw
> To dismember her limbs,
> To break her body with an axe,
> To cut out her tongue with a knife,
> To sever her neck with a sword,
> To burn her frame in fire,
> Or to force her to drink poison
> To do away with her life.

King Aśoka said such things intending to punish Tiṣyarakṣitā. When Kuṇāla heard these words, he had a mind of deep compassion and uttered the following stanza:

> 147b What Tiṣyarakṣitā has done
> Are nothing but evil deeds.

Now may the great king
Not kill her for that reason.
None of the great virtues
Can surpass forbearance.
As the World-honored One has said,
It is the first and foremost.

King Aśoka did not listen to his son's words but put Tiṣyarakṣitā into a *lakuca* house and set it on fire to burn her to death. He also issued an order to kill that man of Takṣaśilā.

At that time, a *bhikṣu* was doubtful about the matter and inquired of the most virtuous Upagupta, "What deed did Kuṇāla do in a past life, so that he is suffering this retribution in the present?" The virtuous monk said in reply, "Elder, listen. Long, long ago in the past, there was in the country of Vārāṇasī a hunter who killed many deer in the Snow Mountains. Once when he went to the Snow Mountains a thunderbolt crashed in the sky, and five hundred deer, being frightened by the bolt, fled into a cave. Upon seeing this group of deer, the hunter caught every one of them. Then he thought in his mind, 'If I kill all of them, their flesh will become rotten. I have no other choice but to extract both eyes from each of them, so that they will neither die nor run away, and I can gradually slaughter them afterwards.' Having reflected in this way, he gouged out all their eyes. Elder, what do you think? That hunter was Kuṇāla in a former life. Because he had extracted the eyes of the deer, he was always born in hells for innumerable years. When he was released from the hells and was born in the human world, his eyes were always extracted for five hundred lives. His present life is the last residue of his retribution."

The *bhikṣu* inquired again, "What was the cause of his being born into an eminent clan with a pair of handsome eyes and gaining arhatship?"

"Elder, listen," said [Upagupta] in reply. "Long, long ago in the past at a time when the span of human life was forty thousand years, a Buddha, a fully enlightened one, by the name of Krakucchanda appeared in the world. When that Buddha had done all he ought to have done in this world, he entered perfect nirvana. There was then a king by the name of Śubhavyūha, who constructed a stupa with the four precious substances for that Buddha, the World-honored One. After the king's demise, his younger brother, who did not believe in the Buddha, secretly took away the jewels and gems with which the stupa was built, leaving only the earthwork and the wooden structure behind. All the people who saw that the stupa was damaged cried with regret and annoyance.

"The son of a householder asked the people, 'Why are you crying with regret and annoyance?' They said in reply, 'Originally the stupa for the World-honored One had the four precious substances, but now they are destroyed and gone! Thus we are crying with regret and annoyance at the sight.' The son of the householder restored the stupa with the four precious substances as it was before and enlarged it so that it was broader and higher than it was at the beginning. He also made a golden image and placed it
147c in the stupa. After having done this, he made a vow, saying, 'As Krakucchanda is the teacher of the world today, may my future teacher be the same as this Buddha now.' You should know, *bhikṣu*, that that son of a householder was Kuṇāla. As the result of his mending and repairing the stupa of Krakucchanda Tathāgata, he was born into a prominent clan in this life. Because he made an image of the Tathāgata, his body in the present life is most handsome and graceful. And as he vowed to meet a good teacher, he now has Śākyamuni as his teacher and realizes the four noble truths."

Chapter V

The Causes of Offering Half an *Āmra* Fruit to the Sangha

Having acquired firm faith, King Aśoka asked the *bhikṣus*, "Who has made the largest amount of offerings ever to the cause of the Buddha-dharma?" The *bhikṣus* said in reply, "The Elder Anāthapiṇḍada gave the largest amount of offerings." The king asked again, "What amount of offerings was he able to give to the cause of the Buddha-dharma?" The *bhikṣus* said in reply, "He spent a hundred crores of taels of gold." Having heard this, King Aśoka reflected, "If the Elder Anāthapiṇḍada could spend a hundred crores of taels of gold, I should also spend a hundred crores of taels of gold in alms giving."

King Aśoka constructed eighty-four thousand stupas and offered one hundred thousand taels of gold each to the place where the Buddha was born, the place where he attained the Way, the place where he turned the Wheel of the Dharma, and the place where he entered nirvana, and also to each of the places where the various arhats entered nirvana. He also convened a great assembly of the four groups of Buddhist followers. He offered food at the same time in one day to three hundred thousand monks, of whom one-third were arhats and two-thirds were learners and zealous ordinary people. Again, King Aśoka, retaining only his treasures, offered all his land, palace attendants, ministers, and Kuṇāla, as well as himself, to the Sangha. He also presented four hundred thousand taels of gold in alms to the Sangha and paid an enormous amount of gold to redeem his land and his own person. Later, he offered ninety-six crores of taels of gold to the Sangha in alms.

When King Aśoka was afflicted with a serious illness, he was very sad and worried. Upon hearing that the king was ill, the minister Rādhagupta, who was the king's friend and rejoiced at his good deed of offering sand as alms in a previous life, went to the king's place and saluted him at his feet. And then he uttered the following stanza:

148a Your face formerly resembled a lotus,
That no dust or filth could stain.
All enemies of great strength
Could never get sight of the king,
Who was like the hot sun at the meridian
Upon whose rays nobody could gaze.
How is it that today
You are shedding tears and sadly sobbing?

King Aśoka answered with the following stanza:

Now I am sad and worried,
Not for the sake of my life or wealth
But because I shall leave the group of saints—
For this I am sad and worried.
All the disciples of the World-honored One
Have achieved various kinds of merits.
With different sorts of food and drink,
I make daily offerings to them.
As I remember this matter,
I cannot help shedding tears.

"Moreover, Rādhagupta, formerly I desired to offer one hundred crores of taels of gold to the Three Treasures, but my intention was not fulfilled. Now I intend to present forty [*sic*] crores of taels of gold in alms to satisfy my original intention." After due consideration, he wished to send forty crores of taels of gold to Kukkuṭa Monastery.

At that time, Kuṇāla's son Saṃpadin was the crown prince. The minister said to the prince, "King Aśoka will pass away very soon, and yet he wishes to send forty crores of taels of gold to

Kukkuṭa Monastery. As all kings depend on wealth for their power, the prince should order the treasure keeper not to allow the gold to be taken out." Thus the prince issued the order accordingly, and the edict of King Aśoka was not put in force. But golden vessels were provided for the king to take his meal. After taking his meal, he ordered that the golden vessels be sent to Kukkuṭa Monastery. Thus golden vessels were withheld, and silver ones were allowed for his use. After taking his meal, the king again ordered that the silver vessels be sent to Kukkuṭa Monastery. So silver vessels were withheld, and iron ones were provided for the use of the king. But after taking his meal, he again ordered that they be sent to Kukkuṭa Monastery. Then iron vessels were also withheld, and earthenware vessels were allowed for his use. Then King Aśoka had nothing more in his possession except half an *āmra* (mango) fruit in his hand. As King Aśoka was greatly distressed in his mind, he summoned his ministers and people and said to them all harmoniously, "Who is now the lord of this earth?" The ministers rose up to salute him and said with folded hands, "Only heaven and nobody else is the lord." Then King Aśoka shed tears that rolled down like rain, and he uttered the following stanza:

I, King Aśoka of today,
Have no more sovereignty
And only half an *āmra* fruit
At my own disposal.
148b What is the use of wealth and nobility,
Which are like water flowing in the Ganges?
Formerly I possessed the land of the country
And was the foremost rich and powerful man.
Now suddenly poverty has befallen me.
I have no more free control over anything.
All unions and meetings
Are bound to end in separation.
The Tathāgata's words of the true Dharma
Nobody is able to comprehend.
Whatever I decreed in former days

Never met with any hindrance,
Like the mind and thought consciousness,
Which are free under favorable conditions.
But what I order now
Is like flowing water impeded by rocks.
All my foes and enemies
I have subdued in former times.
All the land under the rule of the king
Sustained the poor and those in desolation.
I have no more brilliant light,
Like the moon obscured by the clouds.
I am also like an *aśoka* tree
Whose flowers and leaves are withered.
Such am I, King Aśoka,
In the same poverty and plight.

King Aśoka called an attending minister named Bhadramukha and said to him, "Now I have lost my sovereignty and I wish you to be my last messenger. This is the only thing you should do for me. Send this half an *āmra* fruit to Kukkuṭa Monastery and announce my words, saying, 'King Aśoka worships at the monks' feet. Formerly I possessed the land of the whole of Jambudvīpa, but now I have only half an *āmra* fruit. This is my last alms, which I hope the monks will accept. Although this is a small thing, the beneficial merit of offering it to the monks is great.'" And he also uttered the following stanza:

I was formerly a king of men,
Living with sovereignty in my palace.
Impermanence is the peculiarity of the self,
Which will vanish very soon.
Those who can cure the disease
Are the holy fields of blessedness.
Now I have no medicine.
May you save and help me.
This half an *āmra* fruit
Is my last alms.

Small alms may bring great benefit;
Thus you should accept it.

Under the king's order, the messenger sent the half an *āmra* fruit to Kukkuṭa Monastery. Before the elder monk he offered it to the Sangha and uttered the following stanza with his hands joined palm to palm:

148c The whole earth is under the one umbrella
Of the king's rule without hindrance,
Like the brilliant light of the sun
Shining upon all places.
Of his fancied good deeds
The merit has come to the end,
As the sun, sinking down into the earth,
Has no more brilliant light.
With worship and veneration,
He offers half an *āmra* fruit
As a sign of his merit's termination;
It is his last gift.

At that time, the Elder assembled the *bhikṣus* and said to them, "Now you should cherish a mind of fear. Just as the Buddha has said, it is fearful to see impermanence manifested in other persons. Whoever could bear it without a feeling of abhorrence and abandonment? Why?"

Brave and able to give alms
Was King Aśoka of the Maurya clan,
Who had under his rule the great earth,
Jambudvīpa, under his sovereignty.
His recompense is ended today.
He has nothing more than an *āmra*.
All treasures on the great earth
Were under his protection.
This King Aśoka of today
Gives half an *āmra* in alms.
Ordinary beings of all realms of existence

Are proud of the force of their merit and virtue.
We should tell them about impermanence
To arouse their feelings of abhorrence.

When the monks received King Aśoka's half an *āmra* fruit, they crushed it into pulp and mixed it in soup, which was then served to all members of the Sangha.

King Aśoka said to Rādhagupta, "Who is the king now?" Rādhagupta, saluting him at his feet, said with joined hands, "Heaven is the lord of earth, and nobody else is." King Aśoka, who was then supported by some people, looked around at the four quarters and said toward the place of the monks with his palms joined together, "With the exception of my treasures, I now offer the great earth and even the great sea, together with everything else, to the Sangha." And he also uttered the following stanza:

Water is the garment of the earth;
The seven jewels adorn its surface,
Which supports all living beings
As well as all the mountains.
Now I give up all these things
As alms to the monks.
From the monks I shall gain the fruit;
Thus I am giving them these things as gifts.
By the blessing of this alms-giving,
I do not seek the place of Śakra,
Nor to find pleasure in the heaven of Brahman,
Nor to be the lord of all parts of the earth.
I wish to pray by this blessing
Only for the freedom of my mind,
149a To share the Dharma of the saints,
Which can never be seized by others.

King Aśoka wrote this stanza on a piece of *tāla* leaf and sealed it with the marks of his teeth. Holding this document in his hand, he joined his palms toward the place of the monks and said to them,

"I offer this great earth and everything to the Sangha." After having said so, he passed away.

Then the ministers adorned a hearse with multicolored silk as an offering for the body of the king. After making the offering, they intended to perform the ceremony of enthronement by sprinkling sea water upon the head of the crown prince. Rādhagupta said to the ministers, "The whole great earth has been offered to the Sangha by the great King Aśoka." The ministers said in reply, "Then what shall we do?" Rādhagupta replied, "Formerly King Aśoka desired to offer one hundred crores of taels of gold as alms to the Buddha, the Dharma, and the Sangha. When he had given ninety-six crores of taels of gold, he wished to complete the round figure, but the ministers did not agree with him. As the king was discontented, he offered the whole great earth as alms to the Sangha." Then the ministers took out forty crores of taels of gold to redeem the great earth and performed the ceremony of enthronement by sprinkling sea water upon the head of Prince Saṃpadin.

Saṃpadin's son was Bṛhaspati, Bṛhaspati's son was Vṛṣasena, Vṛṣasena's son was Puṣyavarman, and Puṣyavarman's son was Puṣyamitra. When Puṣyamitra ascended the throne, he assembled the ministers [and asked them], "By what expedient means can I make my name everlasting?" The ministers said in reply, "Your Majesty's surname is derived from King Aśoka, who constructed eighty-four thousand stupas so that the Buddha-dharma did not perish; and his name is still well known. Your Majesty should now construct eighty-four thousand stupas." The king said in reply, "The great King Aśoka possessed a great divine power unsurpassed by anyone. Is there any other means for me to keep my name known forever?"

There was then a Brahman, an adept in incantation but an ordinary person not believing the Buddha-dharma, who said to the king, "There are two causes that may make one's name everlasting. The first is to do evil and the second to perform good deeds. The great King Aśoka constructed eighty-four thousand stupas;

but if Your Majesty were to destroy them now, your name would be everlasting."

When King Puṣyamitra intended to destroy the Buddha-dharma, he arrayed his four divisions of troops and went to Kukkuṭa Monastery. Upon arriving at the gate of the monastery, he heard the roar of a lion. Being greatly frightened, the king returned to the country of Pāṭaliputra. In this manner he went to Kukkuṭa Monastery three times, and each time the same thing happened to him.

When he returned to that country, he assembled the monks of that monastery and said to them, "Now I intend to destroy the Buddha-dharma. Among you monks, there are some who guard the stupas and some who protect the monastery. Each of you
149b should tell me of his own case." All the monks said together, "We all protect the stupas." Then the king executed the Elder monk and killed all the other monks.

At that time, the country of Śākala was under the king's domain. He said to the people of that country that anyone who could get the head of a *bhikṣu* would be rewarded with golden money. In that country there was a monastery by the name of Dharmarāja, in which lived an arhat. A man who intended to get his head said to the king, "There is a *bhikṣu* in that monastery. I wish to take his head and send it to Your Majesty." Having heard this, the king desired to take the head of the *bhikṣu* himself. At that moment the *bhikṣu* was absorbed in the intense contemplation of perfect cessation; and by the power of the contemplation, he was invulnerable to knife, stick, fire, and poison. Since he could not kill the *bhikṣu*, the king went away to some other place and reached the country of Koṣṭhaka. In that country there was a Yakṣa deity who was guarding the Buddha's tooth relic. The Yakṣa reflected, "The Buddha-dharma is going to perish. But as I am observing the precepts, I can no longer kill any living creature. I have a daughter, whom the Yakṣa Kṛmiśa originally wished to marry. But as he often committed evil deeds in former times, I did not give my permission. Now, for the sake of protecting the Buddha-dharma I should give her to him in marriage."

There was another powerful Yakṣa who always protected King Puṣyamitra. Owing to his power nobody could injure the king. The deity who guarded the Buddha's tooth relic led away to the South Sea the Yakṣa who protected the king; and at that moment the Yakṣa Kṛmiśa brought a great mountain and pressed it on King Puṣyamitra and his four divisions of troops, who all died instantly. Thus that mountain was named Sunihita (Well Placed). Since King Puṣyamitra was killed, the great Maurya clan died out.

Chapter VI

The Causes of the Buddha's Prediction Concerning Upagupta

When the Buddha wished to enter nirvana, he converted the Nāga kings Apalāla and Gopālacaṇḍāla; and after having done so, he came to the country of Mathurā. In that country he told Ānanda, "One hundred years after my nirvana, there will be in this country of Mathurā a perfumer by the name of Gupta whose son Upagupta will be a Buddha without the special marks. He will perform the functions of a Buddha and teach many people to achieve arhatship.
149c Into this cave, which is eighteen cubits long and twelve cubits broad, he will ask each of his disciples to put a chip four inches long and thereby eventually fill up the cave. Ānanda, you should know that after me Upagupta will be the foremost in edifying his disciples. Ānanda, do you see that green mountain in the distance?" Ānanda said in reply, "I see it, World-honored One!" The Buddha said, "That mountain is named Urumaṇḍa. One hundred years after the Tathāgata's nirvana, the *bhikṣu* Śāṇakavāsin will build a monastery on that mountain and preach the Dharma to edify Upagupta, who will become a monk. In the country of Mathurā there will be two brothers named Naṭa and Bhaṭa. Being the sons of a wealthy person, they will be donors for the construction of the monastery on Mount Urumaṇḍa. Thus the monastery will be named Naṭabhaṭikā. Ānanda, you should know that this monastery will be the best place for meditation."

Ānanda wondered how Upagupta would benefit so many people. The Buddha said to Ānanda, "You should not wonder at this matter. Even long ago in the past when he was born in an evil path [as a monkey], he already benefitted many people. Again, beside

Urumaṇḍa Mountain on its three sides, there were in the past five hundred *pratyekabuddhas* on one side, five hundred recluses on another side, and five hundred monkeys on the third side. Among the monkeys there was a chief monkey who went to the *pratyekabuddhas*. Being delighted to see them, he picked fruits and flowers from the trees and offered them to the *pratyekabuddhas*. The *pratyekabuddhas* were sitting cross-legged, and the monkey paid homage to them one by one. After having worshipped them, the monkey sat erect at the last seat after the monks, and he did so every day. When all of the *pratyekabuddhas* entered nirvana, the monkey did not know it and made offerings to them as before. When he saw that the *pratyekabuddhas* did not accept his offerings, he dragged their clothes and pulled their feet, but the *pratyekabuddhas* did not move. Then the monkey realized that all the *pratyekabuddhas* were dead. He cried and wept sorrowfully, and went to the recluses.

"The five hundred recluses were lying on thorns and thistles, and the monkey, imitating the recluses, also lay on thorns and thistles. He also imitated the recluses by lying on ashes and earth and scorching himself with heat from five directions as the recluses did. When they had gone away after scorching themselves, the monkey quenched the piles of fire with water and hid the ashes away. He pulled up the thorns and thistles on which the recluses had lain and threw them away. He also cleared away the ashes on which they had lain. The recluses grasped the branches of trees to suspend themselves in the air. The monkey loosened their hands and made them drop to the ground. He often taught the recluses how to behave themselves in the four respect-inspiring forms of demeanor in walking, standing, sitting, and lying. After having taught them this, he sat upright before them to practice concentration and said to them, 'All of you should sit like this.' The five hundred recluses then sat together with him in
150a meditation. Having no teacher to preach the Dharma to them, the recluses meditated on the thirty-seven classified ways leading to enlightenment and attained the path of the *pratyekabuddha*. Having attained the path, they reflected, 'It is owing to this

monkey that we have attained the holy path.' Thus they offered incense, flowers, food, and drink to the monkey. When the monkey came to the end of his life, the *pratyekabuddha*s cremated his body with fragrant wood."

The Buddha said to Ānanda, "That monkey was Upagupta. Even in an evil path of existence, Upagupta did great benefit for many people. One hundred years after my nirvana, he will again perform great beneficial deeds on Mount Urumaṇḍa."

At that time, the World-honored One said to Ānanda, "Hold a corner of my robe." Then the World-honored One lifted Ānanda's physical body into the air, and they went together to the country of Kaśmīra. Upon arriving there, [the Buddha] said to Ānanda, "Do you see the many mountains and forests here?" Ānanda said in reply, "I see them, World-honored One!" He again told Ānanda, "One hundred years after my nirvana, there will be in this country of Kaśmīra the *bhikṣu* Madhyāntika, who will establish the country of Kaśmīra in this land." Then the Buddha gradually proceeded to the city of Kuśinagara. When the time of his nirvana arrived, he told the Elder Mahākāśyapa, "Now I wish to enter nirvana. You should collect the Dharma-*piṭaka*, to make it last one thousand years in order to absorb and convert all living beings." Mahākāśyapa said to the Buddha, "World-honored One, I shall act according to the instructions of the World-honored One."

The Buddha then thought of Śakra. Being aware of the Buddha's mind, Śakra, the Lord of Devas, came to the Buddha. The World-honored One told Śakra,"Kauśika, you should protect and maintain the Dharma-*piṭaka*." Śakra said to the Buddha, "World-honored One, I shall do so." The World-honored One then thought of the Four Heavenly Kings, who, knowing the mind of the Buddha, came to the Buddha. The Buddha said again to the Four Heavenly Kings, "After my nirvana, the four of you should protect and maintain the Dharma-*piṭaka*. Even in the future, during the times of the three wicked kings, you four together should protect and maintain the Dharma-*piṭaka*." The Four Heavenly Kings said to the Buddha, "We shall do so, World-honored One!"

At that time, having entrusted the Dharma-*piṭaka* to Mahākāśyapa and Śakra as well as to the Four Heavenly Kings, the World-honored One returned to the country of Mathurā, gradually proceeded to the twin *sāla* trees in the city of Kuśinagara, and told Ānanda, "The time of my nirvana is approaching. Make a bed for me to the north of the twin *sāla* trees. At midnight tonight I shall enter perfect nirvana." And he also uttered the following stanza:

Bottomless is the sea of birth and death,
With waves and deep whirlpools.
Old age and sickness are the shore
From which I have crossed the sea.
150b Intending to enter the land of no sorrow,
I give up this body as a raft.
Rebirth is like the sea,
With fearful old age as its water.
Śākyamuni is the bull king
Who has crossed the sea of rebirth,
Like a man depending upon a raft
Who safely reaches the other shore.

This has been extensively related.

After the Buddha's nirvana, eight stupas were erected to preserve his relics. The ninth stupa contained a water pot and the tenth one was a stupa of embers. Thus a stanza was uttered as follows:

Eight stupas were as tall as mountains,
Relics were preserved underneath.
The ninth one was a stupa of the water pot,
And the tenth one a stupa of embers.

Śakra, the Lord of Devas, and the Four Heavenly Kings offered all kinds of incense and flowers as well as different kinds of music to the relics, and he said, "The World-honored One entrusted us with the Dharma-*piṭaka* and entered nirvana. Now we should comply and protect the Buddha-dharma." Then Śakra said to Dhṛtarāṣṭra,

"You should protect the Buddha-dharma in the east." He said to Virūḍhaka, "You should protect the Buddha-dharma in the south." He said to Virūpākṣa, "You should protect the Buddha-dharma in the west." And he said to Kuvera, "You should protect the Buddha-dharma in the north."

The World-honored One said, "After my death three wicked kings will come to live among you. If they destroy the Buddha-dharma, you should defend and protect it."

Then the Buddha entered nirvana along with innumerable arhats. A sorrowful voice was heard in the air, uttering the following stanza:

> What a pity that the disciples of the Buddha
> Have all entered nirvana.
> Today in this world
> Everything is empty and void.

The shadow of ignorance darkened the lamp of the right Dharma. All the arhats of great virtue entered nirvana. Nobody was there to guard and protect the Buddha-dharma any more, and [it seemed that] the right Dharma of the Tripiṭaka would not last long.

At that time, Śakra and the Four Heavenly Kings as well as countless divine beings went together to Mahākāśyapa. Upon arriving there they worshipped at Kāśyapa's feet and said, "The World-honored One has entrusted the Dharma-*piṭaka* to you, Most Virtuous One, and to us. Most Virtuous One, you should now protect the Buddha-dharma together with us. All the Buddha-dharma should be collected and must not be allowed to disperse. Now the Buddha-dharma, supported and accepted by divine beings and men, will stay in the world for one thousand years for the sake of absorbing and converting all living beings."

Then Kāśyapa struck a bell; and by his supernatural power the sound issued from his mouth, telling all people in Jambudvīpa about it. There were then five hundred arhats staying at Kuśi-
150c nagara. Kāśyapa said to the Elder Aniruddha, "Now who is absent from the assembly of arhats?" Aniruddha said in reply, "Gavāṃpati is now at the Śirīṣa Palace in heaven. He is absent at

the moment." The most virtuous Kāśyapa asked the *bhikṣus*, "Who is the youngest person in this assembly?" The arhat Pūrṇa said in reply, "I am the youngest one." Mahākāśyapa said to him, "Can you accept the instructions of the Sangha?" Pūrṇa answered, "I can." Kāśyapa said again, "Good man, it is excellent, truly excellent, that you can accept the instructions of the Sangha. Now you may go to the Śirīṣa Palace in heaven, to Gavāṃpati, and tell him, 'Mahākāśyapa and the monks summon you to come down. There is a function of the Sangha to be done. You must come quickly.'" And he also uttered the following stanza:

You may go, good man,
To the wood of Śirīṣa.
Leave us here and go
To Gavāṃpati.

Pūrṇa then went to the Śirīṣa Palace and said to Gavāṃpati, "Kāśyapa and the monks who are living in perfect harmony in Jambudvīpa have a function of the Sangha that requires you to go down in haste." Gavāṃpati said in reply, "Good man, you should say the Buddha and the monks instead of Kāśyapa and the monks. Why? Because, the Buddha having entered nirvana, the heretics and the like might despise the Buddha-dharma, and moreover some evil *bhikṣus* might try to cause a schism in the Sangha. The heretics might say, 'Since the Buddha has entered nirvana, the Dharma has also completely disappeared, and the *bhikṣus* know nothing of it.' Formerly when the Buddha was in the world, his light of wisdom made the world bright and brilliant. Now he is dead, and the world has become dark. What is the use of my going there?" He also uttered the following stanza:

The whole world is now empty;
Nowhere is delightful anymore.
Without the Tathāgata to preach the Dharma,
There is nothing to be done in Jambudvīpa.
Now I wish to stay here
To enter nirvana.

"Now you may return there and tell them my mind, saying, 'Gavāṃpati worships Mahākāśyapa and the monks,' and repeat the above stanza."

> The whole world is now empty;
> Nowhere is delightful anymore.
> Without the Tathāgata to preach the Dharma,
> There is nothing to be done in Jambudvīpa.
> Now I wish to stay here
> To enter nirvana.

151a After having said these words, Gavāṃpati entered nirvana.

When Pūrṇa returned to Jambudvīpa, he uttered the following stanza:

> Superior Sangha of great virtues:
> The venerable Gavāṃpati
> Said with veneration:
> "Since the Buddha has entered nirvana,
> Today I shall also
> Enter nirvana.
> Just as when the great elephant died,
> His son followed suit."

At that time Mahākāśyapa made a rule: From then onward all monks should live in harmony to collect the Dharma-*piṭaka*. Until this function was completed, none of the *bhikṣus* should enter nirvana. And he also uttered the following stanza:

> From today onward
> All monks should live in harmony.
> As long as the Dharma-*piṭaka* is not collected,
> None should enter nirvana.

When the five hundred arhats were living in harmony, Mahākāśyapa informed the Sangha, saying, "This Elder Ānanda has always followed the Tathāgata. He is getting old now, and all monks should respect him." He also uttered the following stanza:

This Elder Ānanda
Received and upheld what the Buddha said.
He is sharp-witted and has intelligence
And always followed the Tathāgata's steps,
Understanding the Buddha-dharma with a pure mind.
Thus we should respect him,
As he is beneficial to all monks
And is praised by the One with Ten Powers.

At that time, Mahākāśyapa said to the *bhikṣus*, "If we collected the Dharma-*piṭaka* at this place, many monks would come here in crowds and would certainly weep with grief, which would disturb our Dharma function. We should go to the country of Magadha, where the Buddha attained enlightenment, to collect the Dharma-*piṭaka*."

Kāśyapa and the five hundred arhats then went to the city of Rājagṛha, while Ānanda, supported by the Elder Vṛjiputra, travelled to the country Vṛji. When they arrived there the four groups of devotees of that country were sad and grieved to hear that the Buddha had entered nirvana. At that time Ānanda reflected, "If the four groups are upset and grieved in their minds, how can I preach the Dharma?" The Elder Vṛjiputra thought in his mind, "I should observe the mind of the *upādhyāya* (teacher) to see whether he is a saint or an ordinary person." Then he found that the *upādhyāya* still had a mind attached to learning and was not free from the world of desire. Having seen this, he went to Ānanda, and upon reaching there, he uttered the following stanza:

You should go under a tree
To fix your mind on nirvana.
While Gautama was sitting in meditation,
Very soon he attained nirvana.

151b At that time, the Elder Ānanda, under the edification of Vṛjiputra, spent the whole day in walking and sitting to wash his mind of the five covers. He did so from the first till the fifth watch in the night; and when Venus appeared, he went out to wash his feet. Having washed his feet, he returned to the monastery and intended to lie down with his right side on the bed. Before his head touched the pillow, he freed himself from all passions and attained arhatship.

Then he went to the city of Rājagṛha where Kāśyapa and the five hundred arhats had also arrived. At that time, Ajātaśatru, son of Vaidehī, on hearing that Kāśyapa and five hundred arhats were coming, decorated the road and prepared different kinds of offerings to welcome Mahākāśyapa.

King Ajātaśatru had formerly achieved the rootless faith caused by the Buddha; for when he saw the Buddha coming to him, he prostrated himself from a lofty storied house; but the Buddha took hold of him by his supernatural powers. This time, while he was riding on an elephant, he also prostrated himself at the sight of Mahākāśyapa; and Mahākāśyapa also took hold of him by his supernatural powers. Kāśyapa said to King Ajātaśatru, "The Tathāgata could utilize his supernatural powers without a preliminary thought, but a *śrāvaka* must premeditate before he can utilize his supernatural powers. If you prostrate [from such a height] without my being prepared, you might lose your life. From now on never do it again." The king said in reply, "I shall do as you say."

King Ajātaśatru worshipped at Kāśyapa's feet and said to him with his hands joined together, "Most Virtuous One, when the World-honored One entered nirvana, I did not see him. If you, Most Virtuous One, intend to enter nirvana, you must come to see me." Kāśyapa answered, "Let it be so." And he also said to the great king, "We wish to collect the Buddha-dharma in this city." The king said in reply, "From now on till the end of my life, I shall offer robes, food and drink, medicine, and bedding to the Sangha. The monks may stay at Bamboo Grove Monastery." Then Kāśyapa reflected, "This monastery is broad and big and the [resident] *bhikṣus* might cause a disturbance to our function. I should say that it might be good and might not be good. There is a grotto by the name of Pippalāyana. We should go there to collect the Dharma-*piṭaka*." Then Kāśyapa and the five hundred arhats went together to Pippalāyana Grotto. After arriving there, and having properly arranged their lodgings, he said to the *bhikṣus*, "In the future the *bhikṣus* may lose their correct minds. We should work together to collect the *Udāna* and *Gāthā* before midday, and after midday we shall collect the other Dharmas."

Then the five hundred arhats took their seats according to order, and on each seat was spread a *niṣīdana* (mat for sitting).

All the monks thought in their minds which of the three *piṭaka*s they should collect first. Mahākāśyapa said, "We should first collect the Sutras." The monks said again, "Who can recite the Sutras?" Kāśyapa said in reply, "The Elder Ānanda is the foremost among the well-instructed disciples. All the Sutras were received
151c and retained by him. We should ask him to recite the Sutras." Kāśyapa then said to Ānanda, "You should now recite the Sutras; and we, the assembly, shall collect them together." And he uttered the following stanza:

You, Elder Ānanda, should know
That this Dharma-*piṭaka*
Was created by the Tathāgata,
And that it subsists through your effort.
You uphold the Buddha's Dharma-*piṭaka*,
Like a bull carrying a heavy burden.
The Tathāgata, possessing the ten powers,
Is the peerless and great brave one.
He could put an end to the three realms of being;
And the Buddha-dharma is as fine as clarified butter.
All persons who upheld the Dharma-*piṭaka*
Have already entered nirvana.
You are now the only person
Who has retained the Buddha's Dharma-*piṭaka*.

At that time, the Elder Ānanda said in reply, "Let it be so." Then he rose from his seat, and standing before the presiding Elder and looking at all the monks, he uttered the following stanza:

In this auspicious assembly of monks,
The World-honored One alone is absent.
The mind of purity is unadorned,
Like the sky without the moon.

The Elder Ānanda worshipped the monks one by one, beginning with the presiding Elder. After worshipping them, he ascended the high seat and thought, "Some Sutras I heard personally from the Buddha and some I did not. But now I shall say, 'Thus have I heard' to all of them." The most virtuous Kāśyapa said to Ānanda, "Elder, you should tell us where the Sutras were spoken." And he uttered the following stanza:

> All the great wise ones request
> You, a son of the Buddha, to tell us
> At which place the Buddha's
> First Sutra was spoken.

Ānanda answered, saying, "He spoke the first Sutra for the five *bhikṣu*s in the country of Vārāṇasī. Thus have I heard: Once the World-honored One was staying at the Deer Park of the recluses in the country of Vārāṇasī. The Buddha told the *bhikṣu*s about the noble truth of suffering, and so on." Such as this was extensively related.

At that time, the Elder Ājñātakauṇḍinya reflected, "Among this assembly I am the [only] person who heard this Sutra spoken to me and my companions. The Buddha-dharma that has been transmitted uninterruptedly is the Dharma I heard at the beginning." Thus a sad and regretful feeling arose in him, and upon seeing this sight Ānanda also felt sad and regretful. He came down from the high seat, sat on the ground, and uttered the following stanza:

> The three realms of beings are powerless,
> Like the moon's reflection in the water,
> 152a Or illusion, or the trunk of a banana tree.
> But with the power of wisdom,
> One may know everything in the world.
> Thus one should forsake birth and death
> And try to realize nirvana,
> Like a tree falling in a gale.

At that time, all five hundred arhats left their seats and sat on the bare ground. Kāśyapa said to the *bhikṣu*s, "How is the

Sutra recited by Ānanda?" Then the five hundred arhats entered *samādhi*, and after emerging from *samādhi*, they said, "Such is the Sutra! Such is the Sutra!"

Then the four divisions of the Sutras were extensively recited, and after the collection of Sutras was completed, the monks said, "Now we wish to collect the Vinaya-*piṭaka*, but whom shall we ask to help us do so?"

The most virtuous Kāśyapa said in reply, "The Elder Upāli is foremost in observing the disciplinary rules. We shall ask him to collect the Vinaya as we wish." Then Kāśyapa said to Upāli, "Elder, you should recite the Vinaya, as we wish to collect it." "Let it be so," was the reply. "Where did the Buddha speak about the *pārājikas*?" Upāli said in reply, "In the country of Vṛji." "To whom were they spoken?" "To Sudinna Kalandakaputra." Such things as this were extensively related.

After the collection of the second Dharma-*piṭaka* was completed, Mahākāśyapa again thought, "We ourselves should recite the Mother of Wisdom [i.e., the Abhidharma-*piṭaka*]." Kāśyapa then said to the *bhikṣus*, "What are [the subjects of] the Mother of Wisdom? They are the four objects of meditation, the four right efforts, the four supernatural powers, the five sense organs, the five spiritual powers, the seven branches of enlightenment, the eightfold right path, the four unhindered wisdoms of eloquence, the wisdom of non-disputation, and the wisdom of vows, which should all be collected. The Dharmakāya, the theory of discipline, calmness and tranquillity, and doctrinal views are teachings of the Mother of Wisdom." Thus the most virtuous Kāśyapa concluded the collection of the Dharma-*piṭaka*. And he uttered the following stanza:

> We have collected the Dharma, the Sutras,
> For the benefit of the world.
> The things said by the Buddha of the ten powers
> Were immeasurable.
> The darkness of ignorance in the world
> Can be dispelled by the lamp of the Dharma.

At that time, the Elder Ānanda thought, "When the Buddha, the World-honored One, was about to enter nirvana, he said to those who had violated minor rules that [these rules] might be given up. I should now tell the monks." Then before the presiding elder he said with hands joined palm to palm, "I personally heard the Buddha saying that thenceforward if anyone violated the minor rules, he might give them up and not pretend to observe them. If the monks agree, we may give them up together. When there are no more minor offenses, all the monks may live in peace and happiness."

Then the most virtuous Kāśyapa said to Ānanda, "Did you ask the World-honored One which are minor rules that might be given up and which are not minor rules that might not be given up? Among the five sections [of the disciplinary rules], do they belong
152b to the fifth or the fourth section?" Ānanda said in reply, "I really did not ask. Why? Because all the great *bhikṣus* in the presence of the Buddha did not ask about it, and as I was the youngest person, and had nothing to feel guilty or shameful about in my mind, I did not ask about it. Moreover, as the Buddha was about to enter nirvana, I was feeling sad and sorry, and thus I did not ask about it." Mahākāśyapa then said to Ānanda, "You are guilty of a *duṣkṛta* offense, as you offered muddy water to the Buddha when the Tathāgata asked for water from you at the time of his approaching nirvana." Ānanda said in reply, "I was the youngest person and had nothing to feel guilty or shameful about in my mind. At that time five hundred carts had just crossed the Krakuṣṭha River. I fetched the water shortly after the carts had gone away, and thus the water was muddy." Kāśyapa said again, "When the Tathāgata needed water, why did you not hold the bowl toward heaven, so that heavenly beings would have certainly poured water into it? Why did you fetch muddy water to offer to the Buddha? Therefore you have committed a *duṣkṛta* offense. Again, the World-honored One had a new robe, as yellow as gold in color. Why did you tread on it with your feet?" Ānanda said in reply, "I did not do so out of shamelessness, but because nobody else was there [to help me]. Thus I stepped on it with my foot." Kāśyapa said again, "Why did

you not hold the robe toward heaven? Heavenly beings would have come to hold it. Therefore you have committed a *duṣkṛta* offense. Again, at that time the Buddha said to you that if a man had cultivated the four supernatural powers, he could live for a *kalpa* or less than a *kalpa*, and he let you know that the Buddha, the Tathāgata, had already achieved the four supernatural powers. Why did you not ask the Buddha to stay in the world for a *kalpa* or less than a *kalpa*?" Ānanda said in reply, "Most Virtuous Kāśyapa, I was not shameless. At that time the king of Māras bewitched my mind, and thus I failed to ask the Tathāgata to stay." Kāśyapa said, "That is also a *duṣkṛta* offense. Again, why did you show the Tathāgata's physical mark of a well-retracted male organ to women?" Ānanda said in reply, "It was not out of shamelessness that I showed the physical mark of a well-retracted male organ to women. At that time the women were full of lustful desire, and if they saw the Tathāgata's physical mark of a well-retracted male organ, they would feel disgusted with their female form and wish to gain the male form. That is why I showed it to them." Kāśyapa said, "You have committed a *duṣkṛta* offense for which you should make a confession."

At that time, Kāśyapa said to the *bhikṣus*, "We should now recite the seven rules for settling disputes and other minor offenses." Among the *bhikṣus* some said that the [hundred] regulations to be learned by the monks and nuns were minor rules; others said that the four *dharmas* [concerning public confession] were minor rules; some others said that the ninety rules [about atonement] were minor rules; still others said that the thirty rules [concerning confiscation and expiation] were minor rules; and some others even said that the two rules concerning uncertain cases of infringement were minor rules. Some of them said, "If only the four grave prohibitions and the thirteen rules [concerning temporary expulsion] were reserved while all the other rules were abandoned, the heretics would say that the Dharma of the *śramaṇa* Gautama is
152c motley and variegated. When the Buddha was in the world, the Dharma was harmonious and in unison, and when he passed away, the Dharma also disappeared. After the Buddha's nirvana, all

his disciples acted on their own discretion; those who wished to observe the rules observed the rules, and those who wished to abandon the rules abandoned the rules."

The Buddha said these words, "If a *bhikṣu* cannot observe the disciplinary rules with a whole mind, he should observe them with a right mind. If he has received the disciplinary rules, he should not abandon them but should accept and observe all that the Buddha has spoken. If a *bhikṣu* accepts and observes what was spoken, the good Dharma will increase without retrogression." Therefore all the disciplinary rules spoken by the Buddha were accepted and observed.

Chapter VII

The Causes of the Transmission of the Dharma-*piṭaka* by the Five Disciples of the Buddha

The World-honored One transmitted the Dharma-*piṭaka* to Mahākāśyapa and entered nirvana; Mahākāśyapa transmitted it to Ānanda and entered nirvana; Ānanda transmitted it to Madhyāntika and entered nirvana; Madhyāntika transmitted it to Śāṇakavāsin and entered nirvana; Śāṇakavāsin transmitted it to Upagupta and entered nirvana; and Upagupta transmitted it to Dhītika.

When Upagupta was edifying his disciples in the country of Mathurā, each of them was asked, at the time of becoming an arhat, to throw a chip four inches in length into a cave twelve cubits broad and eighteen cubits long. [Upagupta] made a vow that when the cave was filled with chips he would enter nirvana; and when the cave was full of chips, he did enter nirvana, after having handed over the Dharma to his disciple Dhītika, who was the last disciple to throw a chip into the cave to make it full. Upagupta said to Dhītika, "Formerly the Buddha handed over the Dharma-*piṭaka* to Mahākāśyapa, Mahākāśyapa handed it over to Ānanda, Ānanda handed it over to Madhyāntika, and Madhyāntika handed it over to my *upādhyāya*. Now I hand this Dharma-*piṭaka* over to you." Having handed down the Dharma-*piṭaka*, he entered nirvana seven days later. Both heavenly and human beings passed the news from place to place throughout Jambudvīpa. One hundred thousand arhats came harmoniously together to make offerings, and the number of learners and
153a *upāsakas* and *upāsikās* was uncountable. At the time of entering nirvana, [Upagupta] rose into the air in the postures of walking,

standing, sitting, and lying down, with water coming out of the upper part of his body and fire from the lower part in eighteen transformations. All the heavenly beings and people in the world were delighted. Then he performed *jhāpita* (cremation) of himself with the chips [from the cave]. At that time one thousand arhats entered nirvana with him. Then Dhītika received and protected the Dharma-*piṭaka*.

The Causes of Kāśyapa

The causes of the nirvana of the Elder Mahākāśyapa: At that time the Elder Kāśyapa had all the Sutras, the Vinaya, and the Abhidharma recited. With the wisdom of vows he understood the Tripiṭaka, achieved the body [for his own enjoyment], and realized the *samādhi* of cessation. With the all-comprehensive four unhindered wisdoms of eloquence, he collected the Dharma-*piṭaka* with five hundred arhats. The Dharma as spoken by the Buddha was handed down to various superior persons one by one, so that it might spread to all places for constant reading and reciting and not be lost, for the benefit of all people. He often thought, "I am getting advanced in age, but old age and death are the law of impermanence." He also thought in this way: "I have received according to my ability what the Buddha has spoken. My good friends have received the Sutras, and thus the sons of the Dharma have been born. What I have done at present for requiting the Buddha's kindness is only a small repayment for the Buddha's favors. Who can fully repay all the kindness of the Buddha? All my fellow students are harmonious in the Dharma, and I have been carrying myself too long to receive and gather up the world. I am too tired from carrying myself for so long, and as this stinking body is extremely tired, my time of nirvana is approaching." He also uttered the following stanza:

> We have collected the Sutras
> And have paved the Way.

> We should widely teach the World-honored One's Dharma words
> In all places.

He also uttered the following stanza:

> The shameless ones are expelled;
> Those having a sense of shame are accepted.
> I have done what is beneficial to me.
> My time of nirvana is coming.

Mahākāśyapa then went to Ānanda and said to him, "The World-honored One handed over the Dharma-*piṭaka* to me and then entered nirvana. Now I wish to enter nirvana and hand over the Dharma-*piṭaka* to you. You should accept and uphold it. In due time a son will be born to a merchant in the city of Rājagṛha, and as the child will be born covered with a *śāṇa* (hempen) garment, he will be called Śāṇakavāsin. Śāṇakavāsin will sail on the great sea, and later he will have faith in the Dharma of the World-honored One, to whom he will always make offerings. You should edify him to become a monk and transmit the Buddha's Dharma-*piṭaka* to him."

Mahākāśyapa then handed over the Buddha's Dharma-*piṭaka* to the Elder Ānanda. After having handed over the Dharma-*piṭaka*, he thought in this way: "My World-honored One had great
153b compassion. He did what was hard to do, and his edification was all-round and pervasive. By his countless merits he created his most recent body. The relics of the World-honored One are worshipped at all places. I should enter nirvana, and you ought to know that there is nothing else for me to do." He also uttered the following stanza:

> It was my World-honored One
> Who had great compassion.
> To the relics of the World-honored One
> I have already made offerings.
> It was from him
> That the *samādhi* of enlightenment was born.

To the one who did what was hard to do
This is my last offering.

Mahākāśyapa went by his supernatural powers to the four *caitya*s (shrines) at the places where the Buddha was born, where he attained enlightenment, where he turned the Wheel of the Dharma, and where he entered nirvana. With utmost veneration he worshipped and made offerings to them. He did the same at the eight relic stupas. He also entered the Nāga palace to make offerings [to the Buddha's tooth relic], like a lion king entering a lake that was terrorless, deep, large, unruffled, pure, and undefiled. After having made offerings to the Buddha's tooth relic there, he came out as quickly as the Nāga king could appear in the air and instantly reached the palace of the Trayastriṃśa heaven, where Śakra and the other heavenly beings were glad to make offerings to him. After having received the offerings, he intended to enter nirvana at that place. Upon seeing the signs of the matter, Śakra said to Kāśyapa, "As you are mindful of pure practices, you have always lived in the mountains. What is your intention in coming here? This is a lonely place where you have nobody to depend upon."

At that time, the Elder Mahākāśyapa said to Śakra, "Kauśika, I take pleasure in looking at the Buddha's tooth relic and the Buddha's heavenly crown as well as his *maṇi* (pearl), *pātra* (alms bowl), and other things. This is my last time to make offerings to them." He also uttered the following stanza:

To say that my suffering is ended,
I have come here.
To see the signs of the Buddha,
I have come here.

Śakra and the other heavenly beings, hearing Kāśyapa's words, felt sad and sorry, and out of respect for him they handed the Buddha's tooth relic with both hands to Kāśyapa, who received it respectfully and looked at it without blinking. He offered *mandārava* flowers, *bakula* flowers, and small particles of ox head sandalwood to the tooth relic. Mahākāśyapa said to Śakra and one thousand heavenly beings, "You should practice non-slackness." Then Mahākāśyapa suddenly disappeared from the summit of Mount Sumeru and returned to the city of Rājagṛha.

At that time, the Elder Kāśyapa handed over the Buddha's Dharma-*piṭaka* to Ānanda, and then Ānanda followed behind Kāśyapa every day. Ānanda said to Kāśyapa, "Do not enter nirvana!" Kāśyapa then told Ānanda, "You and I may enter [the city] each by his own way."

153c Ānanda rose early in the morning, and having dressed himself in his robes he took up his begging bowl and entered the city to beg for food. Ānanda was harmonious with others in three delightful ways: first, delightful name; second, delightful listening; third, delightful appearance. People were never tired of looking at him and never tired of listening to him speaking on the Dharma.

Kāśyapa also rose early in the morning, and having dressed himself in his robes, he held his begging bowl and entered the city to beg for food. He thought, "I promised that at the time of entering nirvana, I would go to see King Ajātaśatru." Kāśyapa then went to the royal palace and said to the gatekeeper, "I am here, wishing to see the great king. You may go into the palace to inform the king about it." The gatekeeper said in reply, "The king is now sleeping. I shall inform him after he has awakened." Kāśyapa said, "You may wake up the king." The gatekeeper said in reply, "The king must not be woken up. If he is awakened, he will be greatly enraged; and once he is enraged he will punish me." The Elder Kāśyapa said to the gatekeeper, "When the king has been awakened, you should inform him that Kāśyapa has come here, wishing to enter nirvana. That is why I want to see the king."

Then Kāśyapa went into the city to beg for food. After having begged for food, he went to Kukkuṭa Mountain, which broke into three portions. On the mountain he spread some grass on the ground and pondered, while saying to his own body, "Formerly the Tathāgata covered you with a robe made of cast-off rags. You should stay till the time of the Dharma-*piṭaka* of Maitreya." He also uttered the following stanza:

With my supernatural powers,
I shall keep this body,
Covered with this robe of cast-off rags,
Till the emergence of Maitreya Buddha.
That Buddha, using this body,
May edify his disciples.

At that time Kāśyapa contemplated on three matters. First, after entering nirvana his body should be dressed in his robe of cast-off rags and buried under the three portions of the mountain, like a child in his mother's womb, without being lost or injured, and be kept till the time of the Dharma-*piṭaka* of Maitreya. Second, if King Ajātaśatru comes, the mountain should open. Kāśyapa thought, "If King Ajātaśatru could not see my body, he would vomit hot blood and die." Third, if Ānanda comes, the mountain should open. When he emerged from his contemplation, he forsook his life and entered nirvana. After his nirvana, the earth quaked in six ways. Śakra and innumerable heavenly beings presented various heavenly flowers as offerings to the body of Kāśyapa. The three portions of the mountain closed together to bury his body. As Śakra and the other heavenly beings were separated [from Kāśyapa], they felt sad and regretful, and uttered the following stanza:

We are today
From Kāśyapa far away.
Sad and sorry are our minds,
So much that it is unbearable.
In the Pippalāyana Grotto
All rare Dharmas had arisen.
The people of Magadha
Were born poor and forlorn.
The whole world has nobody
154a To depend upon.
Now this Kāśyapa,
The second Buddha, is extinct.
The right Dharma has collapsed like a landslide;

The ship of the right Dharma is tossing;
The tree of the right Dharma has withered;
The sea of the right Dharma is turbulent;
To the delight of the king of Māras,
Who enjoys this disaster of the Dharma.

After having said this, they suddenly disappeared.

When Ānanda was in the city of Rājagṛha and had not yet come out, Kāśyapa entered nirvana. The Elder Ānanda, having begged for food in the city of Rājagṛha, meditated on impermanence, while King Ajātaśatru dreamed that his maternal clan had perished. He was startled by the dream and awoke in terror. The gatekeeper reported to the king, saying, "Kāśyapa has been here, wishing to see the king. He was going to enter nirvana." Upon hearing these words, the king fainted and fell to the ground. His attendants sprinkled water on him, and when he was recovered a little he went to the Bamboo Grove, where he worshipped at Ānanda's feet. After worshipping him, he stood up and wept sorrowfully, saying, "I have just heard that the Elder Mahākāśyapa has entered nirvana." Ānanda said in reply, "The Great Strenuous One has entered nirvana."

At that time, King Ajātaśatru said to Ānanda, "Let me see Kāśyapa's body; I wish to make offerings to it." Ānanda then took the king to Kukkuṭa Mountain. Ānanda saw that many Rākṣasas (demons) were guarding the body of Kāśyapa. King Ajātaśatru saw the same, and he also saw that Kāśyapa's body was covered with heavenly flowers. Having seen this sight, he raised his hands to pat his own head and prostrated himself at full length, like a tree pushed down by an elephant, to worship at the feet of the body. After worshipping the body, he wished to get some firewood to cremate it. At that moment, Ānanda said, "Great King, what do you wish to do?" The king replied, "I wish to burn the body of Kāśyapa." Ānanda said in reply, "Do not burn it! Do not burn it! This body is preserved by divine power. When Maitreya Buddha attains supreme enlightenment, he will come here, surrounded by ninety-six crores of disciples, to take Kāśyapa's body and show it to them. Maitreya will say, 'This Kāśyapa was a disciple of Śākyamuni. He was the foremost in contentment, with few desires, and he also collected the Dharma-*piṭaka* of Śākyamuni.' Then he will utter the following stanza:

> This recluse *bhikṣu* surnamed Kāśyapa,
> A great disciple of Śākyamuni Buddha,
> Whose supreme good views benefitted the world,
> Accepted and upheld the Dharma-*piṭaka* of that Buddha.

"Maitreya's disciples will think, 'In those days, the human body was so small! Was the body of Śākyamuni the same as this or larger?' When Maitreya Buddha sees his disciples, he will say to them, 'The *saṃghāṭī* robe made of cast-off rags in which Mahākāśyapa's body is wrapped was the *saṃghāṭī* robe of Śākyamuni, the World-honored One.' Upon hearing this, his disciples will feel sorry and
154b disappointed, and thus his ninety-six crores of disciples will attain arhatship. They will also achieve the merits derived from the observance of disciplinary rules and moral conduct. They will then build a stupa on top of the mountain."

King Ajātaśatru returned to his city, and the three portions of the mountain closed together and covered the body again. King Ajātaśatru built a stupa to which he offered different kinds of incense and flowers.

The Causes of Ānanda

When the Elder Kāśyapa had entered nirvana, King Ajātaśatru worshipped at Ānanda's feet and said, "Elder, when the Buddha entered nirvana, I did not see him, and when the Elder Mahākāśyapa entered nirvana, I did not see him either. If you, Elder, wish to enter nirvana, I hope you will come to see me." Ānanda said in reply, "Let it be so."

Now Śāṇakavāsin, the lord of merchants, returned from overseas. After storing away his treasures in his house, he went to the Bamboo Grove. The Elder Ānanda was then standing at the door of the preaching hall. Śāṇakavāsin went up to Ānanda, worshipped at his feet, and sat to the side. Śāṇakavāsin then said to Ānanda, "Elder, may it be known to you that I have returned safely from overseas and wish to hold the quinquennial assembly in order to earn merit from the Buddha and all the monks. Where is the Buddha now?" Ānanda said in reply, "The World-honored One has entered nirvana." Upon hearing this, Śāṇakavāsin fainted and fell to the ground, but when his attendants sprinkled water on him he soon regained his senses. Then he said, "Where did the Elder Śāriputra enter nirvana?" And he also inquired where Mahāmaudgalyāyana, Mahākāśyapa, and some others entered nirvana. After making the inquiries, he said again, "Elder, I wish to hold the quinquennial assembly in order to gain merit." Ānanda said, "You may do so as you wish." And he did so, as has been extensively related.

After the conclusion of the great assembly, Ānanda said to him, "Now you have completed the quinquennial assembly in order to gain merit from the Dharma-*piṭaka* of the World-honored One. Today you should absorb and accept the Dharma." Śāṇakavāsin said in reply, "Elder, what will you teach me?" At that time, Ānanda said to Śāṇakavāsin, "You should become a monk in the Dharma-*piṭaka* of the Buddha." Śāṇakavāsin said in reply, "Let it be so." Then the Elder Ānanda made him a monk and ordained him, [binding him] to observe the complete moral precepts through the performance of the ceremony of making one announcement with three responses, all perfectly performed. Śāṇakavāsin also made a great vow, saying, "I shall always wear this *śāṇa* garment till my death."

The Elder Ānanda received and retained eighty-four thousand Dharma teachings, all that the Buddha and the arhats had spoken. Śāṇakavāsin also received and retained them all. He completely possessed the three clear insights and was well-versed in the Tripiṭaka.

At that time, the Elder Ānanda was residing at the Bamboo
154c Grove, and there was then a *bhikṣu* who recited a stanza in the following way:

A man lives up to a hundred years
Without seeing a heron.
Another man lives for only one day,
But he has seen a heron.
This man has much more wisdom and fame
Than the one of a hundred years.

At that time, Ānanda was walking nearby and heard the *bhikṣu*'s recitation. He said to him, "The stanza you are reciting was not spoken by the Buddha. You should say, 'If one man lives for a hundred years without perceiving the rise and fall of things, and if another lives for only one day but perceives the rise and fall of things, this [second] man possesses much more wisdom than the one who lives a hundred years.' Moreover, there are two kinds of people who slander the Buddha. One kind of people are infidels who slander the Buddha out of hatred and resentment. The other kind, though believers, do not properly accept and understand the meanings of the Sutras and are also considered slanderers of the Buddha. Just as a man with no feet and no mouth is useless, these two kinds of people are useless, as they cannot understand the proper meanings of the words *jāti* (rebirth) and *ariṣṭaka* (heron) mentioned in the Sutra." And he also uttered the following stanza:

An ignorant man has no wisdom;
His actions are useless.
If a wise man does not accept the Dharma,
His wisdom is like poison.
By hearing the recitation of right knowledge,
One may gain the fruit of liberation.

The *bhikṣu* who recited the stanza returned to the place of his teacher and said, "Ānanda said, 'The World-honored One spoke thus: "If one man lives for a hundred years without perceiving the rise and fall of things, and if another lives for only one day and perceives the rise and fall of things, the second man is much better than the one who lives a hundred years." The teacher said to his disciples, "Ānanda is getting old. His memory has become poor." And he also uttered the following stanza:

If a man reaches senility,
He loses his power of memory.
His wisdom and vigor
Also grow old.

He also said to his disciple, "Recite as you do. Do not follow his words."

When Ānanda went again to that place, he heard [the *bhikṣu*] reciting the same stanza. The Elder Ānanda said to him, "I have told you, this was not spoken by the Buddha." He answered Ānanda, saying, "My teacher said that Ānanda was getting old and that his memory had become poor." Ānanda reflected and wished to go to the teacher to tell him the meaning. Then he considered the mind of the teacher: Would he accept his words? He saw in his mind that the teacher would not accept the meaning. He thought again: Was there any other *bhikṣu* who could tell the teacher? And he saw that nobody could tell him. Ānanda considered the matter, "If the Buddha were in the world, I would report the matter to him and to Śāriputra, Maudgalyāyana, Kāśyapa, and others. But the Buddha and all the others have entered nirvana. I also wish to enter nirvana. By the power of the Buddha, the Dharma will abide for one thousand years." He also uttered the following stanza:

155a Recluses such as they
Have all passed away.
Now between them and me,
No distinctive mark will there be.
I am now thinking of myself
As a bird wafting in the wind.
They have entered nirvana,
Having cleared all impurities and bonds.
They were lamps in the world
That dispelled the darkness of ignorance.
Of those great energetic ones
Who observed numerous rules and ceremonies,
I am the only one surviving,
Like one tree remaining in a forest.

Then Ānanda enjoined Śāṇakavāsin, saying, "The World-honored One, after having transmitted the Dharma-*piṭaka* to Mahākāśyapa, entered nirvana; and Mahākāśyapa, after having transmitted it to me, entered nirvana. Now I wish to enter nirvana, and you should accept and guard this Dharma-*piṭaka* of the Buddha.

"In the country of Mathurā there is a mountain named Urumaṇḍa. In the country of Mathurā there is a wealthy person who has two sons named Naṭa and Bhaṭa, whom the Buddha predicted would construct a monastery on that mountain. Again, in the country of Mathurā there is a perfumer named Gupta who will have a son named Upagupta. You should edify him to become a homeless monk. He will be a Buddha without the characteristic marks of a Buddha, as was predicted by the World-honored One, who said, 'A hundred years after my nirvana, he will perform the functions of a Buddha.'" Śāṇakavāsin said in reply, "Let it be so."

Having transmitted the Dharma-*piṭaka* to Śāṇakavāsin, the Elder Ānanda rose early in the morning, dressed himself in his robes, and went to the city of Rājagṛha to collect alms of food. He thought, "I promised that at the time of entering nirvana I should go to see King Ajātaśatru." Ānanda then went to the royal palace and said to the gatekeeper, "I am here wishing to see the great king. You may go into the palace to inform the king about it." The gatekeeper said in reply, "The king is now sleeping. I shall inform him after he has awakened." Ānanda said, "You may wake up the king." The gatekeeper said in reply, "The king must not be woken up. If he is awakened, he will be greatly enraged; and once he is enraged, he will punish me." The Elder Ānanda said to the gatekeeper, "When the king has awakened, you should inform him that Ānanda wishes to enter nirvana. That is why I have come to see the king."

Ānanda then went into the city to collect alms. After having collected alms, he reflected, "If I enter nirvana at this place, King Ajātaśatru will not give a portion of my remains to the people of
155b Vaiśālī; and thus the people of Vaiśālī will certainly bear a grudge against King Ajātaśatru. If I enter nirvana in the country of Vaiśālī, the people of Vaiśālī will certainly not give a portion of my

remains to King Ajātaśatru; and thus King Ajātaśatru will also certainly bear a grudge against the people of Vaiśālī. Therefore, I shall enter nirvana in the middle of the Ganges." Then the Elder Ānanda went to the Ganges.

Meanwhile, in his sleep King Ajātaśatru dreamed that the handle of his canopy was broken, but the canopy did not fall down. He was startled by the dream and woke in fear. The gatekeeper reported to the king, saying, "Ānanda has been here, wishing to see Your Majesty. He is going to enter nirvana." Upon hearing these words, the king fainted and collapsed onto the ground. His attendants sprinkled water on him to wake him from unconsciousness. When he had just recovered a little consciousness, he thought, "Where will the Elder Ānanda enter nirvana?"

At that moment, a divine being in the grove said to King Ajātaśatru, "The Elder Ānanda, a prince of the Buddha-dharma, protected the Dharma-*piṭaka* and with a mind of resolve has brought his existence in the triple world to an end. With a quiet and tranquil mind he has gone to the country of Vaiśālī to enter nirvana." King Ajātaśatru then assembled his four divisions of troops—elephants, horses, chariots, and footmen—and proceeded to the bank of the Ganges.

In the country of Vaiśālī there was also a divine being, who uttered the following stanza to the people of Vaiśālī:

> This recluse Ānanda
> Has dispelled the darkness of ignorance.
> To all the multitude of the world
> He shows equally the mind of compassion.
> He has come to the country of Vaiśālī
> With the intention of entering nirvana.

Then the Licchavis of Vaiśālī also assembled their four divisions of troops—elephants, horses, chariots, and footmen—and proceeded to the bank of the Ganges. At that moment, Ānanda was sailing in a boat to the middle of the Ganges, when King Ajātaśatru arrived and saluted Ānanda, uttering the following stanza with his hands joined palm to palm:

The son of the Buddha enters nirvana
With a mind of equality toward the triple world.
The Buddha whose face resembled a lotus flower
Has already entered nirvana.
You are the one under whom we take refuge.
You should never leave us or abandon us.

At that time, the people of Vaiśālī worshipped at Ānanda's feet and said to him, "At this place you are remembered by men and heavenly beings, but now you wish to realize extinction. In this world Gautama was the supreme one with perfect wisdom and with eyes resembling lotus flowers. For the benefit of the forlorn and solitary, you should embrace the world."

The Elder Ānanda thought in this way, "If I enter the country of Magadha, the people of Vaiśālī will be vexed and annoyed. But if I enter the country of Vaiśālī, the king of Magadha will be vexed and annoyed. Today I must think over what is appropriate for me to do." Knowing that it was the proper time, he uttered the following stanza:

May half of the merit of the Dharma
Be given to the king of Magadha;
155c The other half of the merit,
To the masses of Vaiśālī.
Thus the two peoples
May make offerings properly.

When the Elder Ānanda was about to enter nirvana, the earth quaked in six ways. There was then a recluse possessing the five supernatural powers who was living in the Snow Mountains with five hundred disciples. The recluse wondered why the earth quaked, and then he perceived that Ānanda was about to enter nirvana. Thus he went with his five hundred disciples to Ānanda, and upon arriving there he worshipped at his feet and said with his hands joined palm to palm, "I shall obtain from the Elder the Dharma as spoken by the Buddha and become a fully ordained monk to lead a pure life of celibacy."

Then a conception arose in the mind of the Elder Ānanda, "All my disciples should come." When he had this idea in his mind, all of his five hundred disciples, being arhats, came together to the assembly. The Elder Ānanda rotated this earth with his supernatural powers, and the recluse with his five hundred disciples became fully ordained monks. At the first *karman* (act of the ordination ceremony), the recluse and his five hundred disciples attained the fruition of *srota-āpanna*s (those who have entered the stream of holy living); at the second *karman* they attained the fruition of *sakṛdāgāmin*s (those who will be reborn only once more); at the third *karman* they attained the fruition of *anāgāmin*s (those who do not return); and at the fourth *karman* they attained the fruition of arhatship, free from all afflictions. As the recluse and his disciples became monks in the middle of the Ganges, he was named Madhyāntika.

After having done what he wished to do, Madhyāntika worshipped at Ānanda's feet and said these words, "Just as the World-honored One converted Subhadra as his last disciple, and Subhadra entered nirvana before him, you, being my *upādhyāya*, should also allow me to enter nirvana before you, as I do not wish to see my teacher entering nirvana." The Elder Ānanda said to Madhyāntika, "The World-honored One transmitted the Dharma-*piṭaka* to Mahākāśyapa and entered nirvana; and Mahākāśyapa transmitted it to me and entered nirvana. Now I wish to enter nirvana and you should receive and maintain the Dharma-*piṭaka*. The Buddha has said, 'The country of Kaśmīra is the best place for a monastery of meditation. One hundred years after my nirvana there will be a *bhikṣu* by the name of Madhyāntika who will uphold the Dharma-*piṭaka* in the country of Kaśmīra.' Therefore you should take the Dharma-*piṭaka* to that country." Madhyāntika said in reply, "Let it be so."

Having transmitted the Dharma-*piṭaka* to Madhyāntika, the Elder Ānanda manifested his supernatural powers and made eighteen transformations, walking, standing, sitting, lying down in midair, and entering the fire *samādhi*. After the conclusion of the *samādhi*, his body issued rays of various colors—blue, yellow,

red, and white—with flames coming out of the upper part of his body and water flowing from the lower part, or water flowing from the upper part and flames coming out of the lower part. At that time, the body of Ānanda was upright and dignified, like a famous mountain out of which pure water flowed and upon which different kinds of flowers grew. Ānanda reflected that he wished to give half
156a of his body to the king of Magadha and the other half to the people of Vaiśālī. Then, with his supernatural powers, he fulfilled this wish to be an almsgiver. By the Diamond of Wisdom he cut his mountain-like body in two and gave half of it to the kingdom of Magadha and the other half to the people of Vaiśālī.

After Ānanda entered nirvana, King Ajātaśatru and all the heavenly beings venerated one half of his remains, while the people of Vaiśālī venerated the other half. Two stupas were erected, one in the city of Rājagṛha and one in Vaiśālī.

The Causes of Madhyāntika

When the Elder Ānanda had entered nirvana, Madhyāntika thought, "My teacher instructed me to bring the Buddha's Dharma-*piṭaka* to the country of Kaśmīra." Madhyāntika then went to the country of Kaśmīra, where he sat upon a rope couch and thought again, "As this country of Kaśmīra is a possession of the Nāga king, if I do not subjugate him he will not come into my realm. I should enter the *samādhi* of suchness." With the power of the *samādhi* of suchness, he caused the country of Kaśmīra to quake in six ways, so much so that the Nāga king could not rest. Thus the Nāga king came to Madhyāntika, who then entered the *samādhi* of compassion. The Nāga king raised a gale but could not stir even a corner of [Madhyāntika's] robe. Then he started a thunderstorm, but Madhyāntika transformed the thunderstorm with his divine power into heavenly blossoms such as *utpala* (blue lotus), *kumuda* (red lotus), *puṇḍarīka* (white lotus), and other flowers, all of which dropped to the ground. He also tried to injure Madhyāntika with various weapons, which were turned by divine power into heavenly flowers. He also used a big mountain to press onto Madhyāntika, and the big mountain became a heavenly blossom. Then the following stanza was uttered in the air:

> A big wind was blowing,
> But it could not stir a corner of his robe.
> Thunderstorms and weapons were turned
> Into celestial blossoms,
> As snow on a mountain,
> Under the light of sunshine,
> Is melted altogether
> Without any remnant.
> When he entered the *samādhi* of compassion,
> Fire could not burn him;
> Weapons and poisonous injuries
> Could never approach him.

Thereupon, the Nāga king was frightened, and he then went to Madhyāntika and said to him, "Holy man, what do you instruct me to do?" Madhyāntika said, "Give this place to me." The Nāga king said in reply, "It is impossible." Madhyāntika said, "It has been predicted by the Buddha that a most superior place for meditation would be initiated in this land, namely, the country of Kaśmīra." The Nāga king said again, "Is this predicted by the Buddha?"
156b Madhyāntika replied, "It is so." The Nāga king said again, "How much land do you wish to have?" Madhyāntika said, "I wish to have a place as large as a couch." The Nāga king said, "Such I shall give." At that time, Madhyāntika enlarged his couch by supernatural power to the size of a *kuṭaru-navaka* (new tent) covering the great earth. The Nāga king said again, "How many people will follow you?" Madhyāntika said, "There will be five hundred arhats." Again, the Nāga king said, "If there is one less than five hundred arhats, I shall retake the residential place." Madhyāntika wondered whether there would be five hundred arhats in the Dharma-*piṭaka*. Then he perceived that there would be no less, nor even more, than that number. So he answered the Nāga king, saying, "Let it be so."

The Elder said again, "If there are almsreceivers, there must be almsgivers. I shall bring white-clothed lay believers to the country of Kaśmīra." The Nāga king said, "Let it be so."

Madhyāntika then brought a large number of white-clothed lay believers to the country of Kaśmīra, where they founded villages and towns. The lay believers said to Madhyāntika, "How shall we sustain ourselves in this place?" Madhyāntika then, by his supernatural powers, brought the lay believers to Gandhamādana Mountain. After arriving there the lay believers dug *kuṅkuma* (turmeric), which they brought back and planted in Kaśmīra.

At that time all the Nāga kings at Gandhamādana Mountain became angry, and Madhyāntika converted and subjugated them. The Nāga kings asked Madhyāntika, "How long will the World-honored One's Dharma-*piṭaka* stay [in the world]?" Madhyāntika said in reply, "It will last one thousand years." The Nāga kings promised that so long as the Buddha-dharma stayed in the world, they would allow him to stay in their country. Madhyāntika said in reply, "Let it be so."

Madhyāntika brought the turmeric back to the country of Kaśmīra and planted it. While the World-honored One's Dharma-*piṭaka* remained, Madhyāntika widely spread it and manifested various supernatural powers. He studied the Buddha-dharma together with the almsgivers, so as to make them understand and comprehend its meaning. Then he entered nirvana, like a fire extinguished by water, and his body was cremated with ox head sandalwood and other fragrant woods. His *śarīra* were collected, and a stupa was erected for them.

The Causes of Śāṇakavāsin

When the Elder Ānanda had entered nirvana, Śāṇakavāsin went to the country of Mathurā. On the way there was a monastery named Piṇḍavana, in which Śāṇakavāsin spent a night. In the monastery there were two old *bhikṣus*, who were discussing a stanza:

"Non-violation is the first precept;
The best learning is the selection of the Dharma."
The *bhikṣus* believed that
This was spoken by Śāṇakavāsin.

Śāṇakavāsin said to the two *bhikṣus*, "The idea you uttered was not spoken by me. What I said was 'the harmony of the right Dharma.' Elders, once in the past there was a lord of merchants in the country of Vārāṇasī, who intended to sail on the great sea with five hundred traders. On the way they met with a *pratyekabuddha* who was sick. The lord of merchants detained the traders to look after the *pratyekabuddha*, and he personally attended to him with
156c the medicine prescribed by a physician. When the *pratyekabuddha* became a little better, the lord of merchants took out a *śāṇa* garment. It had been rough and coarse but was made soft and smooth by treatment with washing and dyeing. After bathing the *pratyekabuddha*, he offered the garment to him, saying, 'World-honored One, that garment of yours is rough and coarse. May the World-honored One accept mine after taking a bath.' The *pratyekabuddha* said in reply, 'Good man, I am getting old, but I became a monk in this *śāṇavāsa* (hempen garment), and with this garment covering my body I gained the holy Dharma. I shall now enter nirvana in this same garment.' The lord of merchants said, 'Do not enter nirvana. When I return from the sea, I shall offer to you, World-honored One, garments, food, drink, bedding, and medicine so long as you do not enter nirvana. I shall now sail on the sea and cannot stay here.' The *pratyekabuddha* said, 'Now I must enter nirvana. You have done great meritorious deeds, for which you should feel happy.' Then the *pratyekabuddha* showed the eighteen transformations to the lord of merchants; and after showing the supernatural transformations, he entered nirvana.

"The lord of merchants made offerings to the body and made a vow, 'I have performed various meritorious deeds for this *bhikṣu*. With this good root I shall obtain what I ought to obtain.' The lord of merchants at that time was myself. That is why I have met with a supreme teacher who caused me to gain the Way. I wore this *śāṇavāsa* when I became a monk in the Dharma-*piṭaka* of the World-honored One. With this *śāṇavāsa* covering my body, I gained the Way, and with this *śāṇavāsa* covering my body, I shall enter nirvana. I have always worn this *śāṇavāsa*; even when I was a lay believer clad in white I also wore this garment. That was why I was named Śāṇakavāsin. I received full ordination, and after the completion of the fourth *karman* I also received the greater precepts. Even before entering nirvana, I shall always wear this *śāṇavāsa*. That is why again I am named Śāṇakavāsin."

At that time, the Elder Śāṇakavāsin gradually proceeded to the country of Mathurā and went to Urumaṇḍa Mountain, where he sat on a rope couch. On Urumaṇḍa Mountain there were two Nāga kings, who were brothers, followed by five hundred Nāgas. Śāṇakavāsin reflected, "If I do not subjugate them, I shall not be able to edify them." Thus he shook the mountain with his supernatural powers. Being enraged, the two Nāga kings went to the place of Śāṇakavāsin, started a strong storm, and set a fire. Śāṇakavāsin entered the *samādhi* of compassion, which could keep the storm and fire away from his body, and transformed the water and fire into celestial blossoms, namely, *utpala*, *kumuda*, *puṇḍarīka*, and other flowers, which all fell to the ground. The Nāgas again caused a thunderstorm, which was also transformed into celestial blossoms by supernatural powers. They also tried to throw various kinds of weapons at Śāṇakavāsin, and these were again transformed into celestial blossoms. They tried to press
157a Śāṇakavāsin with a big mountain, and he also transformed the mountain into a heavenly flower. Then the following stanza was uttered in the air:

A strong gale and storm
Could not hurt him;
Thundering, lightning, and weapons
Turned into celestial blossoms,
As snow on a mountain,

Under the light of sunshine,
Is melted altogether,
Without any remnant.
When he entered the *samādhi* of compassion,
Fire could not burn him;
Weapons and poisonous injuries
Could never approach him.

Then the two Nāga kings went to Śāṇakavāsin and said to him, "Holy man, what do you instruct us to do?" Śāṇakavāsin said in reply, "I wish to build a monastery on this mountain. You should listen to me." The Nāga kings said in reply, "It is impossible." The Elder said, "Such has been predicted by the World-honored One, who said, 'A hundred years after my nirvana, a monastery with the name Naṭabhaṭikā shall be constructed at the best quiet and calm place on Great Cream Mountain.'" The Nāga kings said again, "Is it predicted by the World-honored One?" The Elder said in reply, "It is so." The Nāga kings said, "If it has been predicted by the World-honored One, we shall listen to you."

Then the Elder meditated and observed whether the almsgivers of Naṭabhaṭikā Monastery had been born or not, and he saw that they had been born. Śāṇakavāsin rose early in the morning, dressed himself in his robes, carried his alms bowl, and went to the country of Mathurā to collect food. After having collected food, he went to the place of the almsgivers Naṭa and Bhaṭa. Upon arriving there, he said to the almsgivers, "Good men, you should give me money, as I wish to build a monastery on Cream Mountain." The two brothers Naṭa and Bhaṭa said to Śāṇakavāsin, "We cannot do it." The Elder said, "The Buddha has predicted that the two of you will construct a monastery on Great Cream Mountain." The two men said in reply, "If it is predicted by the Buddha, we shall construct the monastery." Then the two of them built a monastery on the mountain, fully provided with garments, decorations, and other articles. This monastery was thus named Naṭabhaṭikā.

157b

The Causes of Upagupta

When Śāṇakavāsin had constructed the monastery on Great Cream Mountain, he contemplated whether the perfume dealer named Gupta had been born or not, and he saw that he had been born. He then contemplated whether [Gupta's] son Upagupta, who would, as the World-honored One had predicted, be a Buddha without the characteristic marks of a Buddha and who "will perform the functions of a Buddha one hundred years after my nirvana," had been born or not, and saw that he had not yet been born. With his power in expedients, Śāṇakavāsin taught the perfume dealer to be energetic.

One day Śāṇakavāsin went to [the perfume dealer's] house with a large number of disciples; on another day he went to his house with only one disciple; and on still another day he went to his house alone. Gupta was performing Buddhist functions, and when he saw that Śāṇakavāsin came to his house alone, he asked, "Holy man, why are you alone without any disciple following you?" The Elder said, "I am an old man; how can I have anybody following me? If somebody is energetic and takes delight in becoming a monk, then I shall have a follower." Gupta said, "I take delight in the enjoyment of the five desires at home, and I cannot leave my home to become a monk. But if a son is born to me, he will follow the Elder." The Elder said, "Let it be so! Let it be so! Forever keep this promise and never go back on your word."

A son was then born to Gupta and was named Apagupta. When he had grown up, Śāṇakavāsin went to Gupta and said to him, "Formerly you promised me, 'If a son is born to me, I shall give him to the Elder.' Now a son has been born to you. This son is virtuous. You should allow him to follow me to become a monk." Gupta said, "Now I have only one son. When the second son is born, I shall give him to the Elder." Then Śāṇakavāsin pondered whether this child was Upagupta or not, and he saw that he was not. So he said to Gupta, "Let it be so."

When the second son was born, he was named Dhanagupta. After he had grown up, Śāṇakavāsin went to Gupta and said to

him, "Formerly you promised that when your second son was born you would give him to me. Now that the child is born, you should allow him to follow me to become a monk." Gupta said, "May the Elder not feel displeased. I have two sons to manage my family properties together. I order one to procure wealth and one to
157c safeguard it. If a third son is born, I will give him to the Elder." Then Śāṇakavāsin pondered whether this child was Upagupta or not, and he saw that he was not. So he said to Gupta, "Let it be so."

Then the third son was born, a child with handsome features and very lovable. As his pleasant appearance surpassed that of other men and was second only to that of heavenly beings, he was named Upagupta. When this child had grown up, his father kept him to make a lawful living and gained much profit. Then Śāṇakavāsin went to Gupta and said to him, "Good man, formerly you promised that when your third son was born, you would give him to me. Now that this child is born, you should allow him to follow me to become a monk." Gupta said in reply, "I vowed to order him to make a living. If he gains or loses [profit], he will not be allowed to become a monk. If he neither gains nor loses, he will be allowed to become a monk." Then the king of Māras (the Evil One) caused all the people in Mathurā to purchase his goods, so that he gained profits.

Śāṇakavāsin went to Gupta's place when Upagupta was selling perfume. The Elder said to him, "Do you know what is good and what is bad in your mind and mental activities?" Upagupta said in reply, "I do not know what is good and what is bad in my mind and mental activities." The Elder said, "The mind and mental activities that tally with greed, hatred, and ignorance are bad; and if they tally with non-greed, non-hatred, and non-ignorance, they are good."

At another time the Elder went again to Upagupta and said to him, "Good man, how are your mind and mental activities? Are they good or bad?" He replied, saying, "I do not know what is good and what is bad in my mind and mental activities." The Elder said, "If you wish to know what is good and what is bad in your mind and mental activities, you should accept the Way and eliminate what is bad in your mind and mental activities. I shall do something." Then the Elder made some pills with black and white clay and said to him, "If an evil mind arises, you may take one black pill, and if a good mind arises, you may take one white pill. You should practice the contemplation of impurity and be mindful of the Buddha, as well as meditate on him as has been said."

At that time, Upagupta intended to do good in his mind and mental activities, but he collected many black pills without even a single white one. Then he thought that he should try to get two-thirds black pills and one-third white ones. He thought again that he should get half black pills and half white ones. He further thought that he should get two-thirds white pills and one-third black ones. And he even thought that he should have only a good mind, so that the pills he took were all white ones.

There was then in the country of Mathurā a courtesan named Vasudattā, whose maidservant once went to the place of Upagupta to purchase perfume and received more than she had bought. When she returned, her mistress asked her, "Where did you get so
158a much perfume? Was it not stolen from the trader?" The maidservant said in reply, "The trader named Upagupta is a person of perfect appearance, and he speaks so nicely, while he sells his goods lawfully." When the mistress heard these words, she cherished a mind of lustful desire for Upagupta and ordered her maidservant to go again to his place. "You may tell him that I desire to have enjoyment with him." When the maidservant told this to Upagupta, he said, "You may tell her that this is not the time for me to see her." The maidservant returned and told this to her mistress, who said, "He cannot afford to give me five hundred silver coins, so he would not come." Then she sent again her maidservant to go and tell him, "I need no money. I only need you to come and have enjoyment with me." The maidservant again went to the place of Upagupta and told him this message. Upagupta still answered, "This is not the time for me to see her." Then the son of another rich man went to Vasudattā.

There was then a merchant coming from northern India to the country of Mathurā with five hundred horses and various kinds of merchandise. After his arrival, he inquired of the people of Mathurā, "Where is the most beautiful woman in this country?" The people of the country said in reply, "There is a most beautiful woman whose name is Vasudattā." The merchant said, "I wish to go to her with five hundred silver coins and various precious things." The courtesan, craving the things, killed the rich man's son [her former paramour], put the corpse in a filthy place, and then she enjoyed herself with the merchant. An intimate friend of the rich man's son discovered his body in the filthy place and reported the matter to the king. The king said to him, "You will seize Vasudattā, amputate her hands and feet, cut off her ears and nose, and scatter her body in the wilds." As ordered by the king, her hands and feet were cut off and scattered in the wilds.

Upon hearing that Vasudattā had had her hands and feet cut off and scattered in the wilds, Upagupta thought, "Formerly I did not wish to see her and enjoy the five desires with her, but now I wish to see her and have a look at her hands, feet, ears, and nose." And then he uttered the following stanza:

> In the best of clothes was she formerly clad;
> With different jewels was she decked;
> Such were the things with which
> Her person was adorned.
> One who takes delight in liberation,
> Who wishes to leave the world with detestation,
> Should not go to see her then,
> When she was decked with precious jewels,
> But should go to see her now,
> Without joy and without arrogance.
> 158b Her beauty is in its original form;
> The sight of her arouses disgust and repugnance.

Upagupta, accompanied by a boy holding an umbrella, went into the wilds. The maidservant, in remembrance of her mistress's kindness, stayed beside her to drive away the crows, not allowing them to attack and peck her. The maidservant said to her mistress, "Formerly you sent for Upagupta several times. Is he coming now with a lustful mind?" Upon hearing these words, her mistress said, "My good appearance has now been deformed. It is really a great pain. Now I am on this ground smeared with blood and my whole body is red. Such being my body, how can anyone have a lustful mind at the sight of it?" Then she said to her maidservant, "Collect my hands, feet, ears, and nose and put them in one place, so that he may not see them." The maidservant placed them together and covered them with a piece of cloth. Then Upagupta arrived and stood looking at Vasudattā. When Vasudattā saw Upagupta, she said to him, "Here comes the good holy man. Formerly when my body was capable of enjoying the five desires I sent for you, but you said that it was not the time. Why do you come now when my hands and feet have been amputated and I am in a bloody mire?" And she uttered the following stanza:

> Formerly this body of mine
> Resembled a lotus flower;
> I wore a precious garment
> Of great price for its adornment.
> But devoid of merit
> I could not see you.

"Such as I am now, why do you come? This body of mine is without ornaments and without joy, smeared with blood for scented ointment. It is a sight of horror and pity." Upagupta said in reply, "I have not come with a mind of lustful desire. It is for the sake of contemplating lustful desire and impurity that I have come." And he also uttered the following stanza:

> With various precious garments
> And different kinds of flowers
> You adorned yourself
> And distracted those who saw you.
> All the people who wished to see you,
> But had no wealth,
> Could not see you.
> Now this body of yours
> Is scattered all over the place.

Of all the people,
None has not seen it.
Your beauty has returned to its true form,
Devoid of adornments
And with such a stench.
The corpse is but a skeleton,
Covered with a layer of thin skin,
Filled with blood,
Wrapped in the thin skin,
Stuffed with flesh
And a thousand veins and arteries
Intertwining throughout the body.
Such is corporeality.
Where lies the beauty?
Damsels and maidens
Are outwardly lovable.
When people see them,
Their desire is aroused.
If they know what is inside,
They will attain deliverance.
158c The noble and respected, the mean and low,
All bear alike stinking corpses.
When a fool sees them,
He considers them pure.
When a wise man sees them,
He perceives them as impure.
This foul and filthy body
Is a store of impurity.
With various kinds of incense
It is fumigated.
This body is only abominable,
With dirt, grime, pus, and blood.
Different kinds of garments
Are used for its ornaments.
It is a container of dirt
Washed clean with water.

Fools and sinners
Are attached to it with love.
Those who have heard the good Dharma
As spoken by the Buddha,
Who profess and accept it
With minds delighting in deliverance,
Who enter groves of solitude
Depending on the Way as a raft,
Will cross to the other shore.

Upon hearing these words, Vasudattā deeply feared rebirth, and when she heard about the virtues of the Buddha, she changed her mind and took delight in nirvana. In reply to Upagupta, she uttered the following stanza:

This is so, this is so;
This is as you have said.
You are truly intelligent and wise
And possess great kindness.
You should tell me more now
About the Buddha's wonderful Dharma.

Upagupta then preached the Dharma, namely the four noble truths, point by point. He also contemplated the body, and through the contemplation of the body he realized the detestability of the world of desire. As he himself preached the Dharma, he thoroughly comprehended the four noble truths and attained the fruition of an *anāgāmin*, while Vasudattā attained the fruition of a *srota-āpanna*.

At that time Vasudattā said to Upagupta, "Excellent! Excellent! Mahāsattva (great being), it is by your power that the three evil ways and the places of great sufferings are closed, and that the path leading to heaven and nirvana is opened. Now I take refuge in the Tathāgata, the one worthy of worship and fully enlightened, as well as in his Dharma and Sangha." And she also uttered the following stanza:

I go to take refuge in the Buddha,
The Most Honored One among bipeds,

Whose eyes resemble blue lotuses,
And who is praiseworthy among men and heavenly beings;
And also in his pure Dharma, free from desires;
As well as in the supreme arhat Sangha.

Having made her happy through his preaching of the Dharma, Upagupta returned to his own place, and shortly after his departure Vasudattā died and was reborn in the heavens. At that time, the heavenly beings informed the people of Mathurā that she had been reborn in the heavens. After hearing this, the people made offerings to her remains.

Then the Elder Śāṇakavāsin went to Gupta and said to him, "You should allow Upagupta to follow me and become a monk." Gupta said in reply, "Formerly I promised you that I would ask him to make a living and would allow him to become a monk only if he were unskillful and blunt in business." Then the Elder
159a Śāṇakavāsin, employing his supernatural powers, rendered [Upagupta] unskillful and blunt in business. Upagupta thought that he was unskillful and blunt in measurement and calculation. Śāṇakavāsin went again to Gupta and said to him, "This son of yours has been predicted by the Buddha, who said, 'A hundred years after my nirvana he will perform a Buddha's functions.' You should allow him to follow me and become a monk." Then Gupta allowed him to become a monk.

At that time, the Elder Śāṇakavāsin brought Upagupta to the Naṭabhaṭikā Monastery and made him a fully ordained monk. At the moment of the first *karman*, he got rid of all bondages and attained the fruition of arhatship. Śāṇakavāsin said to Upagupta, "Good man, you have been predicted by the Buddha: 'A hundred years after my nirvana, there will be a *bhikṣu* named Upagupta who will be a Buddha without the characteristic marks of a Buddha and will perform a Buddha's functions.' And he also said that among the Buddha's disciples, you would be foremost in edifying others. Good man, you should perform beneficial deeds for the Buddha-dharma." Upagupta said in reply, "Let it be so!" And Śāṇakavāsin taught him to preach the Dharma.

When all the people of Mathurā heard that a *bhikṣu* named Upagupta, who was a Buddha without the characteristic marks of a Buddha, was going to preach the Dharma, innumerable thousands of people wished to go to listen to him. The Elder Upagupta then contemplated in *samādhi* and saw that when the Buddha preached the Dharma, his audience, consisting of the four groups of devotees, sat in a group shaped like a crescent moon. He contemplated again: In what order did the World-honored One teach the Dharma? And he saw that the order was the taste of desire, the faults of desire, the outlet of desire, the four faiths, and so on, one by one up to nirvana. Upagupta also preached the Dharma in the same way.

At that time, the king of Māras rained pearls on the assembly to distract the minds of the people. As the people in the assembly were distracted, none of them could understand the four noble truths. Upon seeing that the minds of the people were distracted, Upagupta thought to himself, "Who is doing this to distract the minds of the assembly?" Then he found that it was being done by the king of Māras.

On the second day the people who came doubled in number, and Upagupta again preached the true Dharma of the four noble truths point by point. At that time, the king of Māras again rained gold to distract the minds of the assembly, and none of the people could understand the four noble truths. Upon seeing that the minds of the people were distracted, Upagupta thought to himself, "Who is doing this to distract the minds of the assembly?" Then he found that it was being done by the king of Māras.

On the third day the people who came doubled in number, and Upagupta again preached the Dharma, while the king of Māras again rained pearls mixed with gold, to the accompaniment of heavenly music performed by *apsaras* (goddesses). As the people in the assembly were not free from desire, their minds were excited by the sight of the beauties and the sounds of music, and they listened no more to the preaching of the Dharma. The king of
159b Māras then put a garland around the neck of Upagupta. Upagupta thought, "Who is doing this?" He found that it was being done by

the king of Māras. He pondered in his mind, "As this king of Māras always caused disturbance to the Dharma-*piṭaka* of the World-honored One, why did the World-honored One not edify him?" Then he thought to himself, "I may edify him, as the Buddha predicted that I would be a Buddha without the characteristic marks of a Buddha to edify people and convert them." Then he considered, "Is this the right time for me to edify him?" He saw that the time had arrived for the king of Māras to receive edification.

At that time, the Elder Upagupta took three corpses, the first of a dead snake, the second of a dead dog, and the third of a dead man. With his supernatural powers, he transformed the three corpses into garlands and took them to the place of the king of Māras. At the sight of Upagupta, the king of Māras was greatly pleased, [thinking], "Upagupta has accepted my edification." And he stretched his body to receive the garlands. Upagupta tied him up with his own hands, fastened the dead snake on his head, and fixed the dead dog and dead man under his neck. Upagupta said to the king of Māras, "As you first insulted me with unrighteous flowers, now I return [the insult to] you by fastening corpses upon you. Now you are dealing with a son of the Buddha. If you have any supernatural power, show it to me." Just like a gale that agitates the water of the sea into waves but cannot stir Malaya Mountain, so the king of Māras wished to free himself from the corpses but could not do so even though he tried with utmost effort. He was as helpless as a gnat trying to move a mountain. Greatly enraged, the king of Māras rose up into the air and uttered the following stanza:

> If I cannot free myself
> From the corpses on my neck,
> I may be freed by other divine beings
> With powers greater than mine.

The Elder Upagupta also uttered the following stanza:

> You may go to take refuge under Brahman,
> The sun, the moon, and Śakra;
> You may go into fire and the great sea;

The corpses will not be burned, rotted, or loosed.
I have bound these corpses
Tightly on your neck.
It was done by supernatural power,
And none can detach them.

The king of Māras went to Maheśvara and Śakra in the Thirty-three heavens as well as to the Four Heavenly Kings, trying to get rid of the corpses, but he could not free himself from them. Then he went to Mahābrahman. Mahābrahman said to him, "Good man, since this was done by the supernatural powers of a disciple possessing the ten powers, who ever could rid you of them? It is like water that cannot break the shore of a great sea." He also uttered the following stanza:

159c If Snow Mountain is bound
With fibers of lotus root,
It can be lifted up
Without much difficulty.
It is by the power of divinity
That corpses are fixed on your body.
I do not have the ability
To rid you of them.
All the powers possessed
By me and the heavenly beings
Cannot surpass those of the Tathāgata
And his disciples,
As other lights are inferior
To the light of fire,
As the light of fire is inferior
To the light of the sun.

The king of Māras said, "What would you teach me to do? Under whom shall I take refuge?" Mahābrahman said, "You should now go quickly to take refuge under Upagupta. As a man has to stand up from where he has fallen, you have to stand up through his supernatural powers, since your downfall was caused by his supernatural powers." Then the king of Māras realized that the supernatural powers of a son of the Buddha were great. He pondered over the matter and uttered the following stanza:

> If Mahābrahman takes refuge
> In the Buddha, his disciples, and the Dharma,
> Who else can estimate and measure
> The divine powers of the Tathāgata?
> The Tathāgata's divine powers
> Really could have subjugated me.
> But out of pity and compassion
> He did not subdue me.

"Now I have come to know the powers of the Buddha, and it needs no extensive reiteration." He also uttered the following stanza:

> Now I understand
> That the World-honored One is compassionate,
> And that his mind is free from impurities,
> Comparable to a golden mountain.
> Because of my ignorance,
> I disturbed the Buddha everywhere
> And did evil at all places;
> But he did not subdue me by force.

Then the king of Māras, who was the lord of the world of desire, had no place to escape from Upagupta and pondered over the matter. He gave up his arrogance, went to Upagupta, and worshipped at his feet, saying, "Elder, since the time of the Bodhi tree up to the present day, the evils I have committed against the World-honored One are immeasurable and innumerable. Once I caused the Buddha to have no food to eat when he went to the house of a Brahman in the country of Sālā. That was done by me. For the evils I committed, the Buddha did not blame me. Sometimes I changed myself into a dragon, a snake, a wicked demon, or various kinds of fearful things to frighten him, but the World-honored One never blamed me. Elder, today you are pitiless and cause the whole world of heavenly beings and Asuras to blame and sneer at me, making me feel ashamed."

Upagupta said to him, "You are unwise and do not know how to think of things, trying to compare the merit of the compassion of the Tathāgata with that of a *bhikṣu*. It is like comparing a grain of mustard seed with Mount Sumeru, or equating a glowworm
160a with the sun, or taking a scoop of water and putting it on a par with the great sea. The compassion of a *śramaṇa* is not comparable to that of the compassionate Buddhas of the ten quarters. That was why the Buddha could endure the evils you committed." The king of Māras said, "The Buddha had cut off all delusions and dissolved all doubts and had great patience. As I was wicked and had passions, I was always ready to annoy the Buddha. The World-honored One protected me with his compassion. That was why the Buddha did not subjugate me. Elder, you should instruct me."

Upagupta said in reply, "Good man, now listen to me! You committed so many evils and did so many bad things toward the Buddha that unless you cherish a mind of faith and respect for the Tathāgata, you cannot be absolved from your misdeeds. As the Buddha had foresight far into the future, he did not subjugate you." He also uttered the following stanza:

Your mind has lacked deep respect,
But the Tathāgata has initiated it.
From smallness it will increase to greatness
Until you gain the fruit of nirvana.
Of all the evils you have committed,
Only a brief part has been told.
You should wash away the defilement of passion
With the water of the wisdom of recollection.

The king of Māras remembered the Buddha, and the hair on his body bristled like *kadamba* flowers. He also uttered the following stanza:

Many things I did
To vex the World-honored One,
But he was not angry.
I wish to be compared to a son

Whose guilt and faults are forgiven
By his father's pardon.

At that time, the king of Māras spent much time in meditating on the beneficence of the Buddha, and as he remembered the Buddha his mind was cooled down. He worshipped at the Elder's feet and uttered the following stanza:

The Elder today
Has accepted me
And enabled me to revere
The World-honored One.
Now these corpses
Are bound on my neck
As my ornaments.
May the great recluse,
By the power of compassion,
Remove them for me.

The Elder Upagupta said, "If you can make a promise, I shall remove them for you." The king of Māras inquired, "What promise?" Upagupta said, "From now onward you should never annoy *bhikṣus*." The king of Māras said in reply, "Let it be so! Let it be so! But you should teach me how to do it." The Elder answered, saying, "The Dharma-*piṭaka* of the World-honored One should be widely spread, and that is what I am doing." Being amazed, the king of Māras said again, "Teach me how to do it!" The Elder said in reply, "You should know that I became a monk one hundred years after the Tathāgata entered nirvana. I have seen
160b the Dharmakāya of the World-honored One, but I have not seen
his Rūpakāya (physical body). As you are now accepted by me, you should show me the Rūpakāya of the Tathāgata. I now take delight in nothing else except in seeing the body of the Buddha." The king of Māras replied with the following stanza:

We should make an agreement together.
When you see what I appear to be,
The material body of the Tathāgata,

You must not worship me.
Only to the All-wise One
Should homage be paid.
If the Elder paid it to me,
I should be destroyed.
Now I am not qualified
To bear the worship of a holy man,
Just as the bud of an *airāvata* tree
Cannot bear the weight
Of the tusk of an elephant.
Thus we should make this agreement.

The Elder Upagupta said in reply, "Let it be so. I shall not worship you." The king of Māras said again, "Just wait a few moments. I shall enter the grove and transform myself into the form of the Buddha with brilliant golden hues and a halo as bright as sunlight, just as I did once in the past to mislead a wealthy man named Śūra. Such a material body was wonderful. I shall now appear as it, so that all those who see it may have faith with joy." Then the Elder Upagupta said in reply, "Let it be so." And he removed the three corpses, as he wished to see the physical body of the Tathāgata.

Then the king of Māras went into the grove and transformed himself into the body of the Buddha. Having assumed the form of the Buddha, he came out of the grove, just as a woman goes behind a screen to adorn herself and comes out again after having dressed up. The physical form of the Tathāgata was incomparable, and none of the people who saw it was not pleased to see it. It was like a colored painting with different hues.

When the king of Māras had glorified the grove with his transformed body, he also appeared as Śāriputra at the right side and Maudgalyāyana at the left. Again, he appeared as Ānanda holding an alms bowl at the back and as Mahākāśyapa, Aniruddha, Subhūti, and so on, as one thousand two hundred fifty great *śrāvaka*s surrounding the transformed Buddha in a group shaped like a crescent moon. After having made these transformations, he went to Upagupta. Being greatly delighted to have seen the Buddha's physical form, Upagupta rose from his seat and watched the physical form of the Buddha without turning his eyes away from it for a moment. And he uttered the following stanza:

> Impermanence is merciless;
> It ruined the Tathāgata's material form.
> Impermanent was the Tathāgata;
> He dissolved his form and entered nirvana.

Upagupta fixed his attention on the Buddha, and his mind could not part from him. "Now I see this transformed body, and it is the same as seeing the real Buddha." With a concentrated mind, he put his hands palm to palm and uttered the following brief stanza in praise of the Buddha:

160c
> His face is superior to a lotus flower,
> His eyes, better than the bloom of the *utpala*.
> His color outshines a grove of many blossoms
> And also surpasses real gold.
> He is more lovely than the moon;
> His light is brighter than the sun.
> His wisdom is deeper than the sea;
> Steadier than Mount Sumeru is his immovability.
> He walks more gracefully than the king of lions,
> And he blinks more sedately than the king of bulls.

As his mind was filled with joy, he again uttered the following stanza aloud:

> By his deeds of mental purity,
> He has gained this excellent fruit.
> It was created by his own deeds
> And was not made by others.
> For countless and innumerable *kalpa*s
> He cultivated pure deeds of body and speech
> And practiced the six *pāramitā*s perfectly
> As ornaments for his unhindered body.
> All those who see him are overjoyed;
> He is admired even by his enemies.

Now, as I see the Tathāgata,
How can I not feel joyous?

As he was thinking of the Buddha, Upagupta did not sense that it was Māra and prostrated himself at full length at the feet of the king of Māras like a great tree with its roots broken falling on the ground. Being startled, the king of Māras said, "Elder, you should not break your promise." The Elder said in reply, "What promise?" The king of Māras said, "We made an agreement that when I appeared as the Buddha, you would not worship me. Why do you worship me now?" The Elder rose from the ground and replied in a low voice, "I am not unaware that the Tathāgata entered nirvana like fire extinguished by water. But [when] I saw the physical body of the Tathāgata, it was so wonderful that I worshipped it; I did not worship you." The king of Māras inquired, "You prostrated yourself with your head touching my feet; how can you say that you did not worship me?" Upagupta said, "I neither worshipped you nor did I break my promise. Now listen to me. Suppose there is a Buddha image made of clay; the worshipper thinks of it as the Buddha and not as clay. Now, as I see you, I think of you as the Buddha and not as a Māra."

Then the king of Māras ceased to assume the appearance of the Buddha, made offerings to Upagupta, and returned to his own place. Four days later, the king of Māras struck a bell with his own hands to make an announcement to all people: "Those who wish to be reborn in the heavens and attain nirvana should go to Upagupta to seek advice and receive the right Dharma from him. Those who have not seen the Buddha should go to Upagupta." Then the king of Māras uttered the following stanza:

Those who wish to enjoy wealth and nobility
And do not like to live in poverty,
161a Who wish to enjoy heavenly bliss
And the great happiness of nirvana,
Should listen to and accept the Dharma
And ponder over its meanings and main points.

Those who have not seen
The supreme one among bipeds,
The great teacher possessing compassion
Who spontaneously gained the holy Dharma,
Should all go to Upagupta.
He is the man acting as a bright lamp
For this world.

At that time, his voice was heard throughout the country of Mathurā. After Upagupta had subdued the king of Māras, the Brahmans and all the other people in the country of Mathurā went to Upagupta. He was sitting on a lion seat and preaching the Dharma for the congregation without any fear in his mind, like a lion. He uttered the following stanza:

A man without intelligence
Can never ascend the lion seat.
If he ascended the high seat,
He would be deeply struck with great fear.
Only a man as fearless as a lion,
Who can refute the theories of the heretics,
Is competent
To ascend the lion seat.

Upagupta preached the Dharma point by point, namely, the four noble truths, which were first spoken at the beginning. At that time, innumerable people attained the fruition of a *srota-āpanna*, a *sakṛdāgāmin*, or an *anāgāmin*, and eighteen thousand persons renounced their homes and attained arhatship through the practice of meditation and the strenuous cultivation of the Way.

On Urumaṇḍa Mountain there was a cave eighteen cubits long and twelve cubits broad. At that time all the disciples had done what they ought to do, and the Elder Upagupta said to them, "I have taught all my disciples to attain arhatship. Each of you who have attained arhatship should put a chip four inches long into the cave." In one day's time eighteen thousand arhats put chips into the cave. It became widely known throughout the great earth up to the seaside that in the country of Mathurā there lived

Upagupta, who was the foremost in teaching and converting the people as the Buddha had predicted.

The Causes of Śāṇakavāsin's Attainment of the Way

When Śāṇakavāsin had made Upagupta a monk and Upagupta converted and subdued the king of Māras, Śāṇakavāsin thought for the sake of converting living beings, "I have already received the right Dharma, and now I wish to proceed to the country of Kaśmīra to enjoy the bliss of *samādhi*, as it was predicted by the World-honored One that the county of Kaśmīra would be a first-
161b rate place for sitting in meditation." Then Śāṇakavāsin went there and entered a cave to enjoy the bliss of *samādhi*. When a gust of cool wind blew on his body, he realized arhatship and enjoyed the bliss of emancipation. Then he uttered the following stanza:

> Wearing a *śāṇa* garment,
> Keeping contact with five kinds of *samādhi*
> At the best place on the mountain,
> I sit erect in meditation.
> May the voice of the wind
> Announce to the whole of Kaśmīra:
> This person Śāṇakavāsin
> Has gained the bliss of the Way.
> I pledge with my purity
> That I have gained perfect liberation.
> This person Śāṇakavāsin
> Has uttered this stanza himself.

Chapter VIII

The Causes of Upagupta's Disciples

The Causes of the Son of a Tigress

When Upagupta was residing at Naṭabhaṭikā Monastery on Great Cream Mountain in the country of Mathurā, a tigress gave birth to a cub not far from the monastery. As she could not go to seek food, she died of starvation. With a mind of beneficence and compassion, Upagupta fed the cub. Upagupta had five hundred disciples who had not gained the fruition of the Way. They said to their teacher, "Why do you feed a living being born in an unfortunate state of existence?" Their teacher said in reply, "Good men, it is for the cause of its emancipation." Upon hearing these words, his disciples were amazed and had doubts in their minds. "How can a living being born in an unfortunate state of existence acquire the cause of emancipation?"

The cub had a short span of life, and when it was about to die, Upagupta said to it, "All deeds are impermanent, all things are devoid of an ego, and nirvana is quietude. You should have faith in me and abhor the way of rebirth as an animal." Then the cub cherished a mind of faith and respect toward the Elder. After having had faith and respect it died and was reborn among human beings in the country of Mathurā. When he reached the age of seven, he was converted by Upagupta and became a monk, and in
161c seven years he attained arhatship. With his supernatural powers he plucked different kinds of flowers to offer to Upagupta.

Upagupta was surrounded by his disciples as the arhat disciple came through the air and stood before him. The five hundred disciples who had not gained the Way said to their teacher, "This is our schoolmate. He is still young, so how could he have gained the merits of supernatural powers?" Their teacher said in reply, "He was the cub in his previous life, and you asked me why I should feed such a living being as he. It was because he had seen me and heard the Dharma that he gained his present fruition." Then Upagupta preached the Dharma to his five hundred disciples. And so they got a deep sense of shame, cut off their passions, and attained arhatship.

The Causes of Gorasa (Cow's Milk)

In southern India there was a man who became a monk in the Buddha-dharma and always feared rebirth but was unable to attain nirvana. He thought in his mind, "Who can preach the Dharma to edify me? If anybody can preach the Dharma to edify me, I shall attain nirvana." Then he heard that in the country of Mathurā there was a disciple named Upagupta, whom the World-honored One had predicted would be the foremost in edification. Having heard this, he went to Upagupta in the country of Mathurā . Upon reaching there, he worshipped at his feet and said with his hands joined palm to palm, "Elder, the Buddha has entered nirvana. Elder, you should now perform the Buddha's functions and preach the Dharma for me." When Upagupta saw that this was the monk's last reincarnation, that he feared the pains of rebirth, and that he came from a distant place with a thin and extremely weary body, he said, "Good man, rest yourself for a while." The man was used to living on milk and curds, but in the country of Mathurā there was food and drink of every description except milk and curds, so Upagupta asked him to proceed by another path.

On the other path the man met with a group of women carrying milk, curds, beverages, and ghee. They were coming from another country with the intention of entering this country. The women asked the Elder why he was so weak and thin. He said in reply, "Sisters, I was born in southern India and always lived on milk and curds. But in this country of Mathurā there is food and drink of every description except milk and curds, and that is why I am weak and thin." Then, to make him strong, all the women gave him milk, curds, and ghee for several days.

Upagupta then preached the Dharma for him; and he practiced it with diligence and attained arhatship. Upagupta said to him, "Take a chip and put it into the cave." He followed the instruction.

The Causes of a Southern Indian

162a In southern India there was a man who had immoral relations with the wife of another man and often went to her house. His mother, not wanting to allow him to do so, said to him, "If a man commits this evil deed, he will stop at nothing in doing evil." Out of anger, that man murdered his mother; and after committing the crime he went to another country. As he could not satisfy his five desires in that country, he felt so deeply vexed and miserable that he became a monk in the Buddha-dharma. Then he thoroughly mastered the Tripiṭaka and became a man of great erudition. Surrounded by his disciples, he went with them to Upagupta at Naṭabhaṭikā Monastery in the country of Mathurā. Upagupta observed him in contemplation and saw that he had murdered his mother and that on account of this felony he could not perceive the truth or gain the fruit of the Way. Although he came from a distant place, [Upagupta] did not greet him with comfort. The *bhikṣu* then went far away from there with a mind of shame.

Upagupta's five hundred disciples who had not gained the Way witnessed the incident and felt displeased with their teacher. They thought, "The *upādhyāya* is lacking in wisdom. He would preach the Dharma for an old *bhikṣu* with a dull and stupid mind but would not preach for this *bhikṣu* who is clever and intelligent, well-versed in the Tripiṭaka, and followed by his retinue."

Upagupta saw that his disciples harbored a feeling of anger against him, and he also saw that their minds had to be converted and quelled by his *upādhyāya* Śāṇakavāsin. At that time

Śāṇakavāsin was residing in the country of Kaśmīra; and when he observed whether Upagupta was performing the Buddha's functions or not, he saw that his five hundred disciples were indignant with him and did not show respect to their teacher. Having seen this, he reflected, "Why does Upagupta not edify them?" Then he made a deeper observation and saw that they could not be edified by Upagupta and that they should be edified by him.

Śāṇakavāsin went to that monastery by his supernatural powers while Upagupta was rambling outside. Śāṇakavāsin then entered the monastery with a long beard and long hair and wearing a coarse garment. Upon seeing him, the disciples of Upagupta said to him, "Ignorant old man, where did you come from with a long beard and long hair and wearing a coarse garment to our teacher's monastery? Our *upādhyāya* did not preach the Dharma to an intelligent *bhikṣu* well-versed in the Tripiṭaka who came here before. How can he preach it for you, an old and dull man?"

When Śāṇakavāsin entered the monastery, he sat on the seat of Upagupta. Upagupta's disciples were angry at seeing it and tried to drag him off with their hands, but he was as immovable as Mount Sumeru. Then they intended to rebuke him, but they lost their voices. So they reported to Upagupta, saying, "A poor old *bhikṣu* has come into the *upādhyāya*'s monastery and is sitting on the *upādhyāya*'s seat." Upagupta said to his disciples in reply, "Nobody except my *upādhyāya* can sit on my seat." When
162b Upagupta returned to the monastery, he made offerings to his *upādhyāya* Śāṇakavāsin with the utmost veneration and took a small seat, sitting on it beside his teacher. Upagupta's disciples thought, "Perhaps this *bhikṣu* is the teacher of our *upādhyāya*, but his wisdom is not as good as that of our *upādhyāya*." Śāṇakavāsin saw their minds and reflected, "What expedient shall I employ to eliminate their arrogance?" After having seen it, he raised his right arm while milk came out from his hand, and he said to Upagupta, "Good man, what is this *samādhi*?" Upagupta said to his *upādhyāya* in reply, "I do not know the name of this *samādhi*." His *upādhyāya* told him, "It is named the *Samādhi* as Powerful as a Dragon." For a second time, milk came out again, and he asked,

"What is the name of this *samādhi*?" Upagupta said in reply, "I do not know the name of this *samādhi*." His *upādhyāya* said, "It is named the *Samādhi* of Pure Harmony and the [Seven] Phases of Enlightenment." And he also extensively related various kinds of *samādhi*. Upagupta said to his *upādhyāya*, "May the *upādhyāya* speak what is within the scope of my wisdom and not speak what is beyond my scope." Śāṇakavāsin said to Upagupta, "Good man, the name of the *samādhi* that is comprehended by the wisdom of a Buddha is unknown to a *pratyekabuddha*. The name of the *samādhi* that is comprehended by the wisdom of a *pratyekabuddha* is unknown to Śāriputra. The name of the *samādhi* that is comprehended by the wisdom of Śāriputra is unknown to Maudgalyāyana. The name of the *samādhi* that is comprehended by the wisdom of Maudgalyāyana is unknown to Mahākāśyapa. And the name of the *samādhi* comprehended by the wisdom of my *upādhyāya* is unknown to me." Śāṇakavāsin said again, "Good man, at the time of my nirvana, the Dharma of all these *samādhis* will be lost. Moreover, the Jātaka stories of the World-honored One with their seventy-seven thousand names will also be lost. Ten thousand Abhidharmas will be lost, too." When the disciples of Upagupta heard this, they felt sorry and vexed, and then they thought, "The wisdom of this *bhikṣu* is superior to that of our *upādhyāya*." Thus their arrogance vanished. Śāṇakavāsin preached the Dharma to edify the disciples, and all of them attained arhatship.

At that time, the Elder Śāṇakavāsin said to Upagupta, "Good man, the World-honored One transmitted the Dharma-*piṭaka* to Mahākāśyapa and entered nirvana; Mahākāśyapa transmitted it to my *upādhyāya* and entered nirvana; and my *upādhyāya* transmitted it to me and entered nirvana. Now I transmit it to you and shall enter nirvana. You should guard and protect this Dharma-*piṭaka*. In this country of Mathurā, a man will be born with the name of Dhītika. He will become a monk, and you may transmit this Dharma-*piṭaka* to him."

When the Elder Śāṇakavāsin had transmitted the Dharma-
162c *piṭaka* to Upagupta, he rose into the air by his supernatural

powers, appeared in the four respect-inspiring postures, and entered the fire *samādhi*. After the conclusion of the *samādhi*, different kinds of flowers, blue, yellow, red, and white, emerged from his body. Water flowed from the upper part of his body and fire spurted from the lower part. Fire also spurted from the upper part while water flowed from the lower part. His body was as upright and dignified as a mountain, with water coming out from one side and fire from the other. With his various supernatural powers, Śāṇakavāsin made the *bhikṣus* and lay supporters happy and free in their minds. After having made such transformations, he entered nirvana like a fire quenched by water. At that time, Upagupta and eighteen thousand arhat disciples made offerings to the body, for which they built a stupa and a temple.

The Causes of a Northern Indian

When Upagupta was residing at Naṭabhaṭikā Monastery in the country of Mathurā, there was a good man in northern India who became a monk in the Dharma of the World-honored One. He was well-learned and intelligent, and he thoroughly mastered the Tripiṭaka. He preached the Dharma so well and in such a good way that wherever he went he was invited by the people to preach the Dharma. Thus he preached the Dharma in three ways for the people. He often thought to himself, "Who can preach the Dharma for me, so as to enable me to gain the Way?" He heard that in the country of Mathurā there was a *bhikṣu* named Upagupta who was foremost in edification and had been predicted by the Buddha to be a Buddha without the characteristic marks of a Buddha. After hearing this, he went to that country and reached Naṭabhaṭikā Monastery. After arriving at the place where Upagupta was, he said, "The World-honored One has entered nirvana. Elder, you are now performing the Buddha's functions. May you preach the Dharma for me." Then he uttered the following stanza:

The Buddha, who had great compassion,
Has already entered nirvana,
And you are now performing the functions of the Buddha.
For the ignorant, blind, and dull in the world,
You are the light of wisdom,
Illuminating the world like sunlight.
There is no other teacher in the world.
You are the only one to be our teacher,
The best one in edifying disciples.
May the Elder teach and edify me.

Then Upagupta observed the man's mind in contemplation and saw that he was in his last reincarnation and deeply feared rebirth. Why did he not obtain the holy Dharma in his previous incarnation? He saw that it was because the conditions were incomplete. Upagupta provided the conditions to make them complete. He also saw that the man's mind took delight in the bliss of sitting in meditation and did not wish to preach the Dharma. Upagupta said to him, "Good man, if you can accept my instruction, then I shall preach for you." He said in reply, "I shall do so." Upagupta said, "You should preach three kinds of Dharma." He
163a asked again, "What Sutra shall I preach?" Upagupta said, "The five merits of learnedness: (1) the expedient of *skandha*s (aggregates), (2) the expedient of *dhātu*s (spheres), (3) the expedient of *āyatana*s (entrances), (4) the expedient of *hetupratyaya* (cause and subcause), and (5) the preaching of the Dharma for the edification of others, without waiting for teaching from others. Now I have taught you the three kinds of Dharma." Then the monk preached the Dharma according to the sequence, and after having preached the Dharma he attained arhatship. Thus he took a chip and threw it into the cave.

The Causes of Devarakṣita

When the master merchant Devarakṣita, who was in the country of the Nākulas and who always took delight in alms-giving and had faith in the Buddha, intended to sail overseas, he announced like a lion's roar, "If I return safely from the seas, I shall sponsor the quinquennial assembly of the Buddha-dharma." All the heavenly beings heard and remembered his words, and all the people in the country came to know about it, saying, "Devarakṣita, the master merchant, has made a lion's roar, saying, 'When I return from the seas, I shall sponsor the quinquennial assembly of the Buddha-dharma.'"

There was then living in that country an arhat *bhikṣuṇī*. She observed in her meditation whether Devarakṣita would safely return from the seas or not, and she saw that he would safely return. She also saw that after his return he would sponsor the quinquennial assembly of the Buddha-dharma. She again tried to see how many monks would join in the assembly, and she saw that the number would be eighteen thousand arhats, twice as many learners, and innumerable ordinary persons. Who would be the Presiding Elder of the assembly? She saw that the Elder would be named Āṣāḍha. Then she observed whether the Elder Āṣāḍha would be an arhat, an *anāgāmin*, a *sakṛdāgāmin*, or a *srota-āpanna*, and she saw that he would be an ordinary person. She again observed whether that person would be energetic or indolent and saw that he would be energetic. Then she contemplated with the intention of inquiring whether he was acting for his own benefit or for the benefit of others, and she saw that he was acting for his own benefit.

So she went to that monk's monastery, and after arriving there she worshipped the monks in due order and said to the Elder, "Most Virtuous One, you are not in strict propriety." The Elder thought to himself, "Why am I deemed to be not in strict propriety?" When he looked at himself and saw that his beard and hair were long, he asked a young *bhikṣu* to shave his beard and hair. When he had been shaved, the *bhikṣuṇī* thought, "Does this Most Virtuous One understand my words?" Then she saw that the most virtuous monk did not understand the meaning of her words, and so she went again to the monastery, worshipped the monks in due order, and said, "Most Virtuous One, you are not in strict

propriety." The Elder reflected, "I have shaved my beard and hair. Why am I still not in strict propriety?" He looked at himself again and saw that his garments were coarse and shabby, and so he asked a young disciple to have them washed and dyed. After having his garments dyed and tidied, he wore them and sat straight. The *bhikṣuṇī* thought again, "Does the Most Virtuous One understand my words?" And she saw that the most virtuous monk did not understand what she meant. For the third time the arhat *bhikṣuṇī* went to the monastery, worshipped the monks in due order, and said, "Most Virtuous One, you are not in strict propriety." The most virtuous monk said angrily, "I have shaved
163b my beard and hair and have washed and dyed my garments. Why do you say I am not in strict propriety?" The *bhikṣuṇī* said to the most virtuous monk, "How can you think that these are the proprieties of the Buddha-dharma? If you can attain the four fruitions, then they are the proprieties of the Buddha-dharma. Furthermore, Most Virtuous One, the master merchant Devarakṣita has made an announcement like a lion's roar: 'When I return safely from the seas, I shall sponsor the quinquennial assembly of the Buddha-dharma.' Have you heard that?" The most virtuous monk said in reply, "I have heard it." She asked again, "Most Virtuous One, do you know the number of monks who will join in the assembly?" "I do not know," was the reply. Then the *bhikṣuṇī* said of her own accord that the number of monks would be eighteen thousand arhats, twice as many learners, and innumerable ordinary persons. "Most Virtuous One, an ordinary person will be the Presiding Elder and will be the first to receive offerings in the assembly of arhats. Will this be fitting behavior?" Upon hearing these words, the most virtuous monk wept sorrowfully. The *bhikṣuṇī* said, "Why do you weep?" "Sister," answered the monk, "I am getting old. I am not competent to do anything." The *bhikṣuṇī* uttered the following stanza:

> The Tathāgata's Dharma can be perceived
> At no fixed season and occasion.
> If one wishes to obtain liberation,
> He may get the fruit at any moment.

"Again, Most Virtuous One, you should go to Naṭabhaṭikā Monastery, where lives the *bhikṣu* Upagupta, whom the Buddha predicted would be the foremost in edification among his disciples."

Then the elderly *bhikṣu* went stage by stage to Naṭabhaṭikā Monastery in the country of Mathurā. When Upagupta saw that the Elder was coming, he came out to greet him and said, "Most Virtuous One, wash your feet and rest." The *bhikṣu* said in reply, "I do not wish to wash my feet. I wish to see Upagupta." Upagupta's disciples said, "This is Upagupta. He has come to greet you, Most Virtuous One." The *bhikṣu* was glad to hear this and washed his feet. Upagupta edified him and found him some lay supporters to look after his bath, food, and drink with various offerings. He also said to the *karmadāna* (distributor of duties), "Now we have a *bhikṣu* who has gained the two liberations coming to our place of meditation." All of the eighteen thousand arhats entered the place of meditation, while the *bhikṣu* came and sat on the chief seat at the place of meditation and fell asleep. The *karmadāna* took a lamp and placed it in front of him with a snap of his fingers. The *bhikṣu* was awakened and wished to take up the
163c lamp. Then Upagupta entered the fire *samādhi*, and thus all of the eighteen thousand arhats also entered the fire *samādhi*. The *bhikṣu* was glad to see this sight and uttered the following stanza:

> All the *bhikṣu*s are sitting
> Cross-legged on the ground
> Like dragons in coils,
> Brilliant as trees of lamps.

Upagupta edified him by preaching the Dharma, and then the *bhikṣu* strenuously practiced meditation and attained arhatship. Having done what he wished to do, he returned to his own country. Upon seeing that the *bhikṣu* had arrived, the arhat *bhikṣuṇī* went to the monastery and worshipped him, saying, "Most Virtuous One, you are today in strict propriety." The *bhikṣu* said in reply, "Sister, it is all due to your effort."

When the master merchant Devarakṣita safely returned from the seas, he sponsored the quinquennial assembly. At that time, eighteen thousand arhats joined the assembly, and there were twice as many learners and innumerable ordinary persons making strenuous efforts. The most virtuous Elder said the following mystic prayer to Devarakṣita: "*Tāvataḥ yāvantaḥ evaṃbhavantaḥ bhavantaḥ bhaviṣyati.*" [Such as it is now, may it be so in the future.] And he repeated the same prayer at the conclusion of the meritorious quinquennial assembly. Devarakṣita, the master merchant, inquired of the Elder, "The World-honored One has preached various Dharmas. Are they any different from what the Elder has said in *Tāvataḥ yāvantaḥ evaṃbhavantaḥ bhavantaḥ bhaviṣyati*?" The Elder said in reply, "Good man, I said the prayer in consideration of your merits. Once in the past, ninety-one *kalpa*s ago, we were both master merchants and managed a big ship, which we sailed overseas to obtain precious things. When the ship was fully loaded, we sailed back to Jambudvīpa. On the sea we encountered a hurricane, and the ship was blown aground on a sandy beach. We collected sand and built a stupa in honor of Vipaśyin Buddha, the fully enlightened one, and offered precious things to the stupa. At that time the heavenly beings showed us the way and we re-equipped our big ship. The heavenly beings said, 'In seven days there will be a high tide, which will take your ship to Jambudvīpa.' On the seventh day the high tide came and took our ship to Jambudvīpa. On account of our construction of the sand stupa, I was not reborn in the evil ways of existence for ninety-one *kalpa*s, and on account of that cause I was able to attain arhatship, while you were able to make offerings to eighteen thousand arhats and twice as many learners as well as innumerable ordinary persons making strenuous efforts. As you have made offerings to the Three Treasures, I said the prayer: *Tāvataḥ*
164a *yāvantaḥ evaṃbhavantaḥ bhavantaḥ bhaviṣyati*. Moreover, my good man, the pains of rebirth are limitless, and you should renounce your home to become a monk in the Buddha-dharma." Thereupon, Devarakṣita became a monk and attained arhatship.

The Causes of the Brahman with the View That the Ego Is Real

When Upagupta was residing at Naṭabhaṭikā Monastery in the country of Mathurā, there was in Mathurā a Brahman who always held the view that the ego is real. He asked a Buddhist disciple, "Is there any being who can create birth and death?" The Buddhist disciple said in reply, "Brahman, please go to Naṭabhaṭikā Monastery, where a *bhikṣu* named Upagupta is always preaching the Dharma of egolessness." The Brahman went accordingly to that monastery when Upagupta was preaching the Dharma for the four groups of devotees. Upon seeing the Brahman, Upagupta uttered the following stanza of non-ego:

> There is no ego in the world
> And nothing that is mine;
> There is no personality and no life,
> Except the concept of birth and death.

Upon hearing the Dharma of egolessness, the Brahman cut off his view that the ego is real and became a monk at the place where Upagupta was. [Upagupta] then preached the Dharma to him, and through the energetic practice of meditation the Brahman attained arhatship. Having done what was to be done, the Brahman took a chip and put it into the cave.

The Causes of Sleepiness

When Upagupta was residing at Naṭabhaṭikā Monastery in the country of Mathurā, a good man who relied upon him became a monk. However, this man was fond of sleep and would fall asleep even when Upagupta was preaching the Dharma. Upagupta asked him to go to a place of meditation; and he went there and sat cross-legged under a tree, but he still fell asleep as before. With his supernatural powers, Upagupta caused pits one thousand cubits deep to appear at the four sides of the *bhikṣu* to frighten him.

Being startled by the sight of the pits, the *bhikṣu* was awakened from sleep. Upagupta then made a road by magic power for him to follow. The *bhikṣu* followed the road and came to Upagupta, who asked him to go back to the place where he had been sitting. The *bhikṣu* said in reply, "*Upādhyāya*, there are pits one thousand cubits deep there." Upagupta said, "Those deep pits are small; the biggest pits are those of rebirth. They are known as the pits of birth, old age, disease, death, sorrow, grief, suffering, and vexation. If one does not know the four noble truths, one falls into them." The *bhikṣu* then went back to sit cross-legged under the tree in meditation, and as he feared the deep pits he did not fall asleep again. With a feeling of dread he meditated energetically,
164b got rid of all passions, and attained arhatship. Then he took a chip and put it into the cave.

The Causes of the Provisor

When Upagupta was residing at Naṭabhaṭikā Monastery in the country of Mathurā, a good man who was a native of the Eastern Country became a monk in the Buddha-dharma, and as he was able to act as a provisor, whichever monastery he stayed in the *bhikṣus* always asked him to be their provisor. The *bhikṣus* said to him, "If any almsgiver comes to you, you should edify him and ask him to perform meritorious deeds." The provisor was so extremely tired of edifying others that he thought, "Who can preach the Dharma to edify me?"

Then he heard that in the country of Mathurā there was a *bhikṣu* by the name of Upagupta, whom the Buddha had predicted would be foremost among the disciples in edifying others. So he went to that place, and upon arriving there he worshipped at his feet and said, "Most Virtuous One, the Buddha has entered nirvana, and you, Most Virtuous One, are performing the Buddha's functions. May you preach the Dharma to me." Upagupta contemplated and saw that this was [the provisor's] last reincarnation and that he feared rebirth. He contemplated again why he did not gain the Holy Way, and saw that it was because conditions were incomplete. What were the expedients by which to make them complete? If he could act again as a provisor, the conditions would be complete. But he also saw that the man was extremely tired of it and did not wish to act as a provisor.

Upagupta said to him, "Good man, if you follow my instructions, I shall preach the Dharma to you." "Let it be so." Upagupta said, "You should act again as a provisor to the monks." The man replied, saying, "Most Virtuous One, I do not know who are zealous and who are not zealous among the people of Mathurā." The Most Virtuous One said to him, "Can you get up early and go to the country?" "I can," was the reply. The *bhikṣu* also asked, "How many monks are there in this monastery?" The Most Virtuous One said in reply, "There are eighteen thousand arhats, twice as many learners, and innumerable energetic ordinary persons." Then the *bhikṣu* acted as a provisor to all the monks so that they might concentrate their minds on the practice of the Way.

The provisor *bhikṣu* rose up early, dressed in his robes, and with alms bowl in hand went into the country of Mathurā. There was then a wealthy man coming out of the country of Mathurā, and he met the *bhikṣu* on the way. He had never met him before; it was the first time he had seen him. Upon seeing him, he worshipped at his feet, and after worshipping him he asked, "Most Virtuous One, are you coming from a far distance or from somewhere near here?" The *bhikṣu* replied, "I come from the Eastern Country." The wealthy man asked him, "For what business have you come here?" The *bhikṣu* said in reply, "I came to Upagupta with the intention of hearing the Dharma. But Upagupta asked me to be provisor to the monks. I do not know who are zealous and who are not zealous among the people of Mathurā." The wealthy man said, "You need
164c not worry about this matter. I shall be the provisor in your stead. I shall provide all the monks with all their food, drink, clothes, and medicine."

Then the *bhikṣu* and the wealthy man jointly provided food and drink and other things as offerings to the monks for the three months of the retreat during the rainy season. The *bhikṣu* contemplated the merits he had achieved and attained arhatship. So he took a chip and put it into the cave.

The Causes of the Artisan

There was then in the Eastern Country a good man who became a monk in the Buddha-dharma, and as he was a good artisan, wherever he went the monks would ask him to construct monasteries and build houses. As he did so every day without ceasing, he was greatly tired of the task. So he thought to himself, "I wish to sit in meditation and contemplation. The Buddha has said that all *bhikṣus* should sit in meditation to cultivate the Way and should not be lazy and indolent." And he reflected, "Who can preach the Dharma to edify me?" Then he heard that in the country of Mathurā there was a *bhikṣu* by the name of Upagupta whom the Buddha had predicted would be foremost among the disciples in edifying others. So he went to him, worshipped at his feet, and said, "Most Virtuous One, the Buddha has entered nirvana, and you, Most Virtuous One, are performing the Buddha's functions. May you preach the Dharma to me." Upagupta saw that this was the monk's last reincarnation and that he feared rebirth. He contemplated again why he did not obtain the Holy Way and saw that it was because causes were incomplete. What were the expedients by which to make them complete? He saw that if the man acted again as an artisan, the causes would be complete. But he saw that the man was extremely tired of it and did not wish to act as an artisan.

Upagupta said to him, "Good man, if you follow my instructions, I shall preach the Dharma to you." "Let it be so," was the reply. Upagupta said, "If no monastery has been built at a place, you should build a monastery there. The Buddha has said that if one builds a monastery at a place where no monastery has been built, one will gain the merits of purity." The man replied, "Most Virtuous One, I do not know who are zealous and who are not zealous among the people of Mathurā." The Most Virtuous One said to him, "Good man, can you get up early, dress in your robes, and go into the country with alms bowl in hand?" "Yes," was the reply. And so he got up early, took up his alms bowl, and went into the country.

There was then a wealthy man coming out of the country of Mathurā. He met the *bhikṣu* on the way, whom he had never seen before; it was the first time he had seen him. Upon seeing him, he worshipped at the *bhikṣu*'s feet and asked him, "Most Virtuous One, are you coming from a far distance or from somewhere near here?" The *bhikṣu* replied, saying, "I came from the Eastern Country." The wealthy man inquired of him, "For what business have you come here?" The *bhikṣu* answered, saying, "I came to Upagupta with the intention of hearing the Dharma, but Upagupta said to me, 'If no monastery has been built at a place, you should build a monastery there.' But I do not know who are zealous and who are
165a not zealous among the people of Mathurā." The wealthy man said, "Most Virtuous One, you need not worry about this matter. I shall make various preparations for the *bhikṣus*." Then the *bhikṣu* and the wealthy man intended to build a monastery at a place where there was no monastery. Working together with the wealthy man, the *bhikṣu* held a rope to measure the ground. Before the rope touched the ground, he contemplated the merits he had achieved therefrom and got rid of all passions. After having attained arhatship, he took a chip and threw it into the cave.

The Causes of Food and Drink

In the country of Mathurā there was a good man who became a monk at the place where Upagupta was, and as he was greedy for food, he could not gain the Way. Upagupta said to him, "I shall give you some food tomorrow." On the following day he filled a vessel with gruel and placed it together with an empty vessel in front of him, saying, "You may take the food and empty the vessel." He also said, "Cool the gruel and eat it slowly." As the *bhikṣu* was greedy for food, he wished to eat more. So he blew on the gruel to make it cool. This he did once or twice, and then he said to the *upādhyāya*, "I have cooled it down." Upagupta said, "Although you could cool the milk gruel, your mind is hot with the fire of desire and love. You should also cool the heat of your greediness and wash away the heat in your mind with the water of the contemplation of impurity. If you are fond of food and drink, you should consider them as if you were taking [them as] medicine."

When the *bhikṣu* had taken all the gruel, he vomited it and filled up the empty vessel. Upagupta said, "You should eat it up." The *bhikṣu* said to the *upādhyāya*, "This vomit is unclean; how can I eat it?" Upagupta said again, "You should now contemplate that all things are impure like snot and spittle." Then Upagupta preached the Dharma to him, and after hearing the Dharma the *bhikṣu* diligently practiced meditation and attained arhatship. He took a chip and put it into the cave.

The Causes of Contentment with Few Desires

There was a good man in southern India who became a monk in the Buddha-dharma and was contented, with few desires, taking no delight in earthly glory, never rubbing his body with ghee, never bathing in warm water, and never eating ghee, for he was always in fear of rebirth. As his constitution was weak in the four elements, he did not gain the Holy Way. He thought in his mind, "Who can preach the Dharma to me?" Then he heard that in the country of Mathurā there was a *bhikṣu* by the name of Upagupta whom the Buddha had predicted would be the foremost among his disciples in edifying others. So he went to him and worshipped him with hands joined palm to palm, saying, "Most Virtuous One, the Buddha has entered nirvana, and you, Most Virtuous One, are performing the Buddha's functions. May you preach the Dharma
165b to me." Upagupta saw that it was his last reincarnation and that he feared rebirth. He contemplated again why he did not gain the Holy Way, and he saw that he was weak in his four elements, and so he always took delight in crudeness and simplicity and did not

wish for earthly glory. Upagupta said to him, "Good man, you should follow my instructions, and I shall preach the Dharma to you." "Let it be so," was the reply. In order to edify him, Upagupta asked the lay supporters to prepare various foods and drinks and baths for the monks. He also said to a young *bhikṣu*, "You should help this *bhikṣu* to take a bath." The young *bhikṣu* then rubbed the man's body with ghee and bathed him in warm water. At mealtime, different kinds of delicious food were provided for him, and the *bhikṣu* finished all the food. In a few days, when his body had gained strength, Upagupta preached the Dharma to him. Through energetic meditation the *bhikṣu* attained arhatship, and then he took a chip and put it into the cave.

The Causes of the Rākṣasas

In the country of Mathurā there was a man who asked permission of his parents to become a monk. He went to Upagupta, and upon reaching him he worshipped at his feet and said, "Most Virtuous One, may I renounce my home to become a fully ordained *bhikṣu* in the Buddha-dharma? I wish to live a pure life of celibacy in the Dharma of the World-honored One." Upagupta saw that he was bound to his body by affection and said, "Welcome, I shall make you a monk." Having heard these words, that man worshipped at the Elder's feet and intended to go back home. On the way he thought, "If I reach home I might be detained and not allowed to become a monk." Midway there was a Deva temple, and so he went in to spend the night there. Upagupta produced two Rākṣasas by his supernatural powers, one of whom carried a corpse into the temple and the other of whom went in empty-handed. In the temple the two of them contended for the corpse. One said, "I obtained this corpse." The other one also said, "I obtained this corpse." In this manner the two Rākṣasas competed with each other for the corpse without coming to a decision. They asked the man, "Who carried this corpse into the temple?" The man reflected, "If I tell the truth, then the one who came in empty-handed will certainly kill me. If I do not tell the truth, the one who came with the corpse will kill me. But I would rather die than tell a lie." So he said to the devils, "He carried it here." The devil who came empty-handed grasped his arm and intended to eat him, but the devil who came with the corpse helped him to free himself from the grip. The devil [who came in without the corpse] again got hold of his foot and intended to eat him, and the devil who came in with the corpse again helped him to free himself from the hold. In this manner they struggled for a long time until sunrise.

Two days later, the man came to Upagupta, and upon reaching there he was made a monk. He practiced the Way diligently and
165c attained arhatship. Then he took a chip and put it into the cave.

The Causes of the Tree

In the country of south India there was a good man who became a monk in the Buddha-dharma but was bound to his body by a feeling of affection. He rubbed his body with ghee, bathed it in warm water, and nourished it with various kinds of food and drink. As he was so much attached to his body, he could not attain the Holy Way. So he thought, "Who can preach the Dharma to me?" When he heard that in the country of Mathurā there was a *bhikṣu* named Upagupta, who had been predicted by the Buddha to be the foremost among his disciples in edifying others, he went to Upagupta in the country of Mathurā. Upon arriving there he worshipped at his feet and said, "Most Virtuous One, the Buddha has entered nirvana, and you, Most Virtuous One, should perform the Buddha's functions and preach the Dharma to me."

Upagupta saw that this was the man's last body in reincarnation and that he was bound to it by a feeling of affection; and he said, "Good man, if you can accept my instruction, I shall preach it to you." "Let it be so," was the reply. Upagupta then brought him to the mountains, where he produced a big tree by his supernatural powers, and he said, "You should climb up this big tree." The *bhikṣu* then climbed up the tree. Under the tree a large pit one thousand cubits in depth and width was also produced by miraculous power. Upagupta said to the *bhikṣu* again, "Put down your feet one by one." The *bhikṣu* accepted the instruction and put down his feet. He said again, "Let go of one hand." This the *bhikṣu* did as he was instructed. He said again, "Let go of the other hand." The *bhikṣu* said in reply, "If I let go of the other hand, I shall drop into the pit and die." Upagupta said, "You have agreed with me that you will accept all my instructions. Why do you not accept my words now?"

At that moment the affection of the *bhikṣu* for his body vanished, and when he let go his hand and dropped down, he did not see any pit under the tree. Upagupta preached the Dharma to him, and he diligently practiced meditation. Thereupon he attained the fruition of arhatship. Then he took a chip and put it into the cave.

166a

The Causes of a Miser

In the country of Mathurā there was a good man who became a monk at the place where Upagupta was, but he was a great miser. Due to his stinginess he could not gain the Holy Way. Upagupta said to him, "You should practice almsgiving. As you have now become a monk and have obtained the principal matter, there is no need for you to seek anything else. You should also offer the Dharma to others. Even the food and drink you have received in your begging bowl should be given to others as alms. If you cannot give extensively, you should share the food the moment you receive it with the two persons sitting beside you." On account of his illiberality, the man did not share his food with others for one day and even for two days. The two persons who sat beside him were both arhats. Only on the third day, when he had received a large amount of food and drink, did he share it with the two persons. Then Upagupta edified him by preaching the Dharma to him, and through meditation he attained arhatship. Then he took a chip and put it into the cave.

The Causes of the Ghost

Once in the country of Mathurā there was a good man who became a monk at the place where Upagupta was, but he was fond of sleeping. Upagupta preached the Dharma to him and brought him to a forest, where he fell asleep in the course of practicing meditation under a tree. In order to frighten him, Upagupta transformed himself into a ghost with seven heads. Holding the branch of a tree, he suspended the ghost's body in the air before the *bhikṣu*, who was startled from sleep and had a great fear of it. He rose from his seat and returned to his original place, but Upagupta ordered him to go back to the place of meditation. The *bhikṣu* said, "*Upādhyāya*, in that forest there is a ghost with seven heads holding the branch of a tree and suspending its body in the air before me in a very fearful manner." Upagupta said, "*Bhikṣu*, there is nothing fearful in the ghost. What is most fearful is the mind of sleepiness. If a *bhikṣu* is killed by a ghost, he will not enter rebirth, but if he is killed by sleepiness, he will experience endless birth and death." The *bhikṣu* then returned to the place of meditation and saw the ghost again. As he feared the ghost, he dared not sleep. Then the *bhikṣu* diligently practiced meditation and attained arhatship. So he took a chip and put it into the cave.

The Causes of Being Bitten by Vermin

Once in the country of Mathurā there was a good man who became a monk at the place where Upagupta was. Upagupta preached the Dharma to him, and the *bhikṣu* practiced meditation diligently with the intention of just gaining the fruition of a *srota-āpanna*. As he was not indolent in his practice, he might be able to rid himself of the fear of being born in the evil ways of existence and then
166b would be reborn seven times in the heavens and seven times among human beings. Then, after having enjoyed the bliss of men and heavenly beings, he would enter nirvana. Having perceived his intention, Upagupta went with him to the country of Mathurā

to collect alms from house to house. They came to the house of a *caṇḍāla* (outcaste), whose son had gained the fruition of a *srota-āpanna* but suffered from a nasty disease; his whole body was bitten by vermin, and he had foul breath. Upagupta said to his disciple, "Look at this child. Though he is a *srota-āpanna*, he still suffers such pains." And he uttered the following stanza:

Born in the caste of *caṇḍāla*s,
Attached to the pleasures of the three realms,
With vermin biting his body,
He loved pleasure freely, and so
He fell into the pains of the three realms.
Look at this son of the Buddha.
He has gained the Way
And was able to overthrow the three evil ways;
But as he was idle and thoughtless,
He was born in the caste of *caṇḍāla*s.
You should not cherish such an idea
But should meditate upon the pains of the three realms.
In order to free you from such pains,
I am obliged to tell you
That you should be energetic,
So that you may gain freedom.
Birth and death are insubstantial,
Like a grove of banana trees.

The *bhikṣu* inquired, saying, "What were the deeds by which this person attained the stage of a *srota-āpanna* but has to suffer such pains?" Upagupta said in reply, "In a previous life, he became a monk in the Dharma of Śākyamuni Buddha, and he was a *karmadāna* while the monks were sitting in meditation. Among the monks there was an arhat who suffered from such a malignant disease that he scratched noisily. The *karmadāna* said to him, 'Is your body being eaten by vermin so that you are making such a noise?' He took the arhat by the arm and led him out, saying, 'Go to the room for *caṇḍāla*s!' At that time, the arhat said to the *karmadāna*, 'Good man, be diligent and do not stay in rebirth to suffer its pains.' Then the *karmadāna* repented, and after his repentance he attained the fruition of a *srota-āpanna*. So he thought to himself, 'I have now attained the fruition of a *srota-āpanna*, and there is no need to be energetic any more.' The child today is the *karmadāna* of the past. As he scolded the arhat, took him out, and sent him to the place for *caṇḍālas*, he is now receiving the retribution."

When the *bhikṣu* heard about this matter, he had deep fear and cultivated devotion diligently, whereby he attained the fruition of arhatship. Upagupta also converted the *caṇḍāla*'s son, who abhorred the Kāmadhātu (the Realm of Desire) and attained the fruition of an *anāgāmin*. Thereupon he passed away and was reborn in the five Pure Dwelling heavens. A chip was taken and put into the cave.

166c

The Causes of Contemplation on a Skeleton

In the country of Mathurā, there was a good man who became a monk at the place where Upagupta was. Upagupta taught him the contemplation of impurity and so on, and by the contemplation of impurity he suppressed his passions so that they could not arise. He thought that he had done what was to be done and that there was no need to be energetic any more. Upagupta said, "Good man, you should be energetic; do not be idle and negligent." [The monk] said in reply, "I have done what is to be done and have attained arhatship." Upagupta said, "Good man, have you seen the woman wine seller named Stonecutter who lives in the domain of the country of Gandhāra? This woman claims to have gained the Way, just as you do, and says that her passions have been cut off while they are not cut off. This is undue self-conceit. You should observe whether this woman has gained the Way or not." The *bhikṣu* said, "I cannot see her." He wished to go to that country, and his teacher gave him permission.

The *bhikṣu* came within the domain of the country of Gandhāra, where there was a monastery with the name of Earth-stone, and he went into the monastery to take rest. He rose early in the morning, put on his robe, carried his alms bowl, and entered the village to collect food. The wine selling woman took out some food and intended to give it to the *bhikṣu*, but at the sight of the woman his mind was excited by lustful desire. He took some grits and butter out of his own alms bowl to give them to the woman. At the sight of him, the woman's mind was also excited by lustful desire, and she smiled, revealing her teeth. Before touching her body or even exchanging a word with her, the *bhikṣu*'s mind was excited. But when he saw the woman smiling and revealing her teeth, he contemplated impurity and perceived that her whole body was nothing but a skeleton. After making this contemplation, he attained arhatship. Having done what was to be done, he uttered the following stanza:

> An idiot is ignorant;
> On seeing external beauty,
> He craves it with attachment.
> A man who has wisdom
> Perceives the internal ugliness
> And may obtain liberation.
> The ignorant one is bound
> By outward appearance.
> One who is wise is not bound
> By external appearance.
> From now onward this body
> Should be given up as impure.
> Never again on this body
> Add any more ornament.
> Observe the reality of the body,
> And you may gain deliverance.

The *bhikṣu* returned to Upagupta in the country of Mathurā, and Upagupta asked him, "Did you see that woman?" [The *bhikṣu*] said in reply, "I saw her according to the Dharma." Then he took a chip and put it into the cave.

The Causes of Avarice

167a In the country of Mathurā there was a householder who was enormously rich at the beginning but gradually became poor afterwards, having only five hundred silver coins in his possession. He thought in his mind, "I wish to become a monk in order to cultivate the Way in the Buddha-dharma. In case I need medicine and robes after becoming a monk, I may use this money to purchase them." So he went to become a monk at the place of Upagupta and ordered his servant to guard the money every day. Upagupta said, "Good man, according to the Dharma of becoming a monk, one should be contented and with little desire. What is the use of these five hundred silver coins? You should offer them to the Sangha." The *bhikṣu* said in reply, "This is the money for me to buy medicine and the three robes." Upagupta asked him to go into his room, where he produced by miraculous power one thousand silver coins, and said to him, "This money is given to you for buying medicine and the three robes." When the *bhikṣu* heard this, he gave up his five hundred silver coins as alms to the Sangha. Upagupta preached the Dharma to him. The *bhikṣu* then practiced meditation diligently and attained arhatship, and so he took a chip and put it into the cave.

The Causes of a Bamboo Brush

In the country of Mathurā there was a good man who became a monk to cultivate the Way at the place where Upagupta was. Upagupta preached the Dharma to him, and the *bhikṣu* practiced meditation diligently, attaining the fruition of a *srota-āpanna*. So he thought in his mind, "I have overturned the evil ways of existence and have done what ought to be done." Upagupta said, "Good man, you should be energetic; do not be idle and negligent." The *bhikṣu* said in reply, "I have already attained the fruition of a *srota-āpanna* and have overturned the evil ways of existence. I shall not be idle and negligent again but shall be reborn seven times in the heavens and seven times among human beings to enjoy the bliss of men and heavenly beings, and then I shall enter nirvana."

Wishing to arouse his fear [of rebirth], Upagupta rose early in the morning, put on his robe, took up his alms bowl, and went with the *bhikṣu* to the country of Mathurā to collect food from house to house. They came to the house of a *caṇḍāla*, whose son was a *srota-āpanna* but suffered from a malignant ulcer. The physician said to him, "You should brush the ulcer with a bamboo brush to make it bleed, and I shall apply medicine to the wound." Upon hearing this advice, the man brushed his body often every day with a bamboo brush. On seeing this sight, Upagupta showed it to his disciple and said, "Good man, did you see this *srota-āpanna* suffering from such pains?" The *bhikṣu* said in reply, "*Upādhyāya,* what were the deeds that produced such pains?"

Upagupta said in reply, "This person became a monk in the Dharma of right enlightenment of Śākyamuni Buddha. There was then a *bhikṣu* who acted as a *karmadāna* to supervise those who were sitting in meditation. Among the monks there was an arhat who came to sit in meditation at the place for meditation; and as
167b he suffered from scabies, he scratched himself. The *karmadāna* said to him, 'Most Virtuous One, why don't you take a bamboo brush to brush your body so that you can make a noise?' He took him by the hand and led him out of the place for meditation, saying, 'You ought to go to the house of a *caṇḍāla* and not disturb the monks!' The arhat said in reply, 'Good man, you should be energetic; do not be idle and negligent so that you suffer the pains of birth and death.' Upon hearing these words, the *karmadāna* repented before the Most Virtuous One, and when he had repented he attained the fruition of a *srota-āpanna*. The *bhikṣu* then thought in his mind, 'I have overturned the evil ways of existence, and there is no need to be energetic any more.' "

Upagupta said to his disciple, "The *karmadāna* at the place of meditation in a previous life is now this *caṇḍāla*'s son. Because he said to the arhat in his former life, 'Why don't you brush your body with a bamboo brush?' he is now receiving this retribution that requires him to brush his body with a bamboo brush today. In his former life he also said to the Most Virtuous One, 'You should go to the house of a *caṇḍāla*.' Thus he was born in the caste of *caṇḍāla*s in his present life." When Upagupta's disciple heard these words, he had fear in his mind. He practiced meditation diligently and attained arhatship.

Upagupta also preached the Dharma to the *caṇḍāla*'s son, who abhorred the Kāmadhātu. He attained the fruition of an *anāgāmin*, whereupon he passed away and was reborn in the five Pure Dwelling heavens. A chip was taken and put into the cave.

The Causes of Parental Sentiment

In the country of Mathurā there was a householder to whom a son was born; but the child died at the age of one. He was reborn in the house of another householder and died at the age of two. He was again reborn in the house of still another householder and died at the age of three. In this manner he was reborn in a fourth, fifth, sixth, and seventh place. At the seventh place he had lived to the age of seven when a thug kidnapped him and took him to the mountains. Upagupta saw in contemplation that this was the last reincarnation of the child, and in order to convert him he went to the mountains and sat cross-legged. There he produced by miraculous power the four divisions of troops—elephants, horses, chariots, and footmen. As the thug was frightened, he went to Upagupta who, withdrawing his miraculous power, preached the Dharma to him. Upon hearing the Dharma, the thug perceived the four noble truths and became a monk. He practiced the Way in the Buddha-dharma and handed over the child to Upagupta. Upagupta asked the child to renounce his home and preached the Dharma to edify him. Through the diligent practice of meditation the child attained arhatship.

Having gained sainthood, he contemplated and saw that his parents were in great distress. So he returned to his parents and said, "Parents, do not be distressed." On seeing that their son had

come back, the parents were greatly delighted. The child arhat
167c preached the Dharma to his parents until they attained the fruition of *srota-āpanna*s. Then he went to his sixth parents and said to them, "Parents, do not be worried. I was your son, once born and reared by you, and died at the age of six." His parents were greatly delighted to hear this, and when he had preached the Dharma to them, they attained the fruition of *srota-āpanna*s. In this manner he preached the Dharma and edified his fifth, fourth, third, second, and first parents until all of them attained the fruitions of *srota-āpanna*s. Then he took a chip and put it into the cave.

The Causes of the River

In the country of Mathurā there was a good man who became a monk at the place where Upagupta was, and as Upagupta preached the Dharma to him he cultivated himself diligently and attained the four stages of *dhyāna*. When he reached the first stage of *dhyāna*, he had the impression of being a *srota-āpanna*; at the second stage of *dhyāna*, he had the impression of being a *sakṛdāgāmin*; at the third stage of *dhyāna*, he had the impression of being an *anāgāmin*; and at the fourth stage of *dhyāna*, he had the impression of being an arhat. He then became unenergetic. Upagupta said to him, "Good man, be diligent and never be idle and indolent." The disciple said, "I have done what is to be done and have attained the fruition of an arhat."

Then Upagupta, edifying him in an expedient way, said, "Good man, you may go to the country of Central India." The *bhikṣu* went there accordingly, and midway on his journey Upagupta produced by miraculous power five hundred merchants who were making a pleasure trip in the mountains, while he also produced five hundred robbers coming to kill the merchants. The *bhikṣu* was greatly frightened when he saw that the robbers were coming to kill him, and then he thought, "I am not an arhat. If I were an arhat, I would have no fear. I may be an *anāgāmin*."

Among the merchants there was the daughter of a householder who had lost her companion and had no friend. Upon seeing the *bhikṣu*, she worshipped at his feet and said to him, "May the holy person take me along and travel with me." The *bhikṣu* said, "The World-honored One has made a rule that [a monk] should not travel with a woman alone. You may follow me at a distance as far as if I were a lion." Upagupta then produced a big river, and the *bhikṣu*, intending to cross the river, waded through the water at the lower reaches of the stream, while the woman waded through the water at the upper reaches. When the *bhikṣu* saw that the woman was nearly drowning in the middle of the river, he thought, "The World-honored One permitted a monk to drag a woman out of the water when she was about to be drowned; he does not commit an offense thereby." Having thought so, he pulled her out of the water, and when the woman had been pulled out, a lustful desire was aroused in his mind. Then he thought again, "I am not an *anāgāmin*. An *anāgāmin* is free from lustful desire. I may be a *sakṛdāgāmin* or a *srota-āpanna*." When the woman was brought
168a ashore, he thought, "Now I wish to cast away all the disciplinary rules to cohabit with this woman."

Upagupta withdrew his miraculous power and stood before the *bhikṣu*, saying, "Good man, are you an arhat?" At that time the *bhikṣu* repented in the presence of Upagupta, who preached the Dharma to him. The *bhikṣu* practiced meditation diligently and attained arhatship, and then he took a chip and put it into the cave.

The Causes of a Whim in Meditation

In the country of Mathurā there was the son of a householder. Not long after he had taken over the family properties, he said to his parents, "Permit me to become a monk." Upagupta made him a monk and preached the Dharma to him, asking him to go to the mountains to sit in meditation. The *bhikṣu* accepted the instruction and went to the mountains, where he sat cross-legged under a tree. Before becoming a monk, the *bhikṣu* had a wife with regular features, and when he was sitting in meditation, he thought of his former wife. Upagupta transformed himself into the form of the *bhikṣu*'s ex-wife and stood before him. Upon seeing the transformation, the *bhikṣu* said to her, "Why did you come?" The woman said in reply, "You called for me." The *bhikṣu* said, "I was sitting here and never said anything. How could I have called for you?" The woman said in reply, "You called for me mentally while in meditation for enlightenment though not orally." The woman then uttered the following stanza:

A shameful thing is of two kinds,
One is oral and one is in the mind.
Of these two kinds,
A mental shame is worse.
Without awareness in the mind,
There could be no oral utterance.

Upagupta withdrew his miraculous power and returned to his own form, and standing before the *bhikṣu* he uttered the following stanza:

If you were not delighted
To look at that woman,
And did not wish to see her,
You would not think of her.
If you have relinquished desire,
You should take no such delight.
What one has vomited
One should never eat again.

Upagupta further preached the Dharma [for the *bhikṣu*], who practiced meditation diligently and attained arhatship. Then he uttered the following stanza:

The *upādhyāya* has seen reality
And has edified me.
As I venerated him,
I have gained the Holy Way.

Then he took a chip and put it into the cave.

The Causes of the Cowherds

168b Once Upagupta was going to the country of Central India, and on the way there he saw five hundred cowherds. Upon seeing Upagupta, the five hundred cowherds went to him, and Upagupta preached the Dharma to them. When they had heard the Dharma, they perceived the four noble truths. Thus they offered their cows to Upagupta and became monks at his place, practicing the Way. Upagupta preached the Dharma to them, and all of them attained arhatship. They took chips and put them into the cave.

The Causes of the Transformed Person

In the country of Mathurā there was a good man who became a monk at the place where Upagupta was in order to practice the Way. Upagupta preached the Dharma to him, and after having heard the Dharma, he reached the four stages of worldly *dhyāna*. At the first stage of *dhyāna*, he had the impression of being a *srota-āpanna*; at the second stage of *dhyāna*, he had the impression of being a *sakṛdāgāmin*; at the third stage of *dhyāna*, he had the impression of being an *anāgāmin*; and at the fourth stage of *dhyāna*, he had the impression of being an arhat, saying, "I have done what is to be done." And so he became idle and indolent and was no longer energetic. Upagupta said to him, "You should be energetic; do not be lazy and negligent." The *bhikṣu* said in reply, "I have done what is to be done and have even attained arhatship."

Upagupta asked him to go to the mountains to sit in meditation, and he also transformed himself into another *bhikṣu* in order to sit with him in meditation and give him advice. [Upagupta as] the transformed *bhikṣu* taught him the methods of meditation and also asked him, "Who accepted you to become a monk, and who is your *upādhyāya*?" The *bhikṣu* said in reply, "Upagupta is my *upādhyāya*, and he accepted me as a monk." The transformed *bhikṣu* said, "It is a great merit for you to have Upagupta, a

Buddha without the characteristic marks of a Buddha, for your teacher." He also inquired, "What scriptures are you reading and reciting? From the Sutras, the Vinaya, and the *mātṛkā* (Abhidharma) have you gained anything of the Buddha-dharma?" The *bhikṣu* answered, saying, "I have attained the fruition of a *srota-āpanna* and even arhatship." The transformed person asked again, "By which way did you attain them?" The *bhikṣu* said in reply, "I attained them by the worldly way." The transformed person said, "What you have attained is but the way of worldly truth. You have not gained the Holy Way."

Upon hearing these words, the *bhikṣu* was deeply vexed with grief. So he went to Upagupta and said to his *upādhyāya*, "I am but an ordinary person. May the *upādhyāya* preach the Dharma to me." Upagupta accordingly preached the Dharma to him, and through diligent practice of meditation the *bhikṣu* attained arhatship. He took a chip and put it into the cave.

The Causes of Taking No Delight in the Dwelling Place

168c In the country of Mathurā there was the son of a householder. Not long after he had taken over the family properties, he cherished the desire to become a monk and said to his parents, "Permit me to become a monk to practice the Way." His parents said in reply, "We have no child except you. We are still living, so how can you leave us behind to become a monk?" When the son heard what his parents had said he was vexed with grief, and for six days he refused to take food. Then his parents permitted him to become a monk and said to him, "When you have become a monk, you should come to see us frequently." He said in reply, "Let it be so," and went to Upagupta to become a monk. After having become a monk, he thought to himself, "I have previously promised my parents that after becoming a monk I would go to see them frequently." So he said to his *upādhyāya* that he was going to his parents. When he saw that his former wife, who was vexed and despondent on account of him, did not adorn herself with ornaments, the *bhikṣu* said to her, "I shall give up the disciplinary rules and return home." He went again to the place of Upagupta, and after worshipping at his feet, he said, "*Upādhyāya*, I single-mindedly desire to give up the disciplinary rules and return to my own place." Upagupta said, "Good man, do not think so. Wait for some time. I wish to know your intention, and when your intention is satisfied, you may give up the disciplinary rules."

Then he ordered him to go to the country of Mathurā, and he transformed himself into the corpse of the *bhikṣu*'s former wife being carried by four persons out of that country. The *bhikṣu* was then going back to see his parents when he saw a corpse being carried out midway [on his journey]. He asked the corpse bearers, "Who is this person?" They said in reply, "This is the corpse of the wife of so-and-so, the son of a householder, who recently became a monk. She died of vexation and despondence. We are removing it to the *śītavana* (cemetery)." Having heard this, the *bhikṣu* went with them, wishing to see the body. Upagupta caused the corpse to emit many worms and blood. Upon seeing this sight, the *bhikṣu* entered into the contemplation of impurity, and through diligent practice of meditation he attained arhatship. When he had done what was to be done, he went to Upagupta and worshipped at his feet. Upagupta said, "Did you see your wife?" He answered, saying, "I saw her in accordance with the Dharma." Then he took a chip and put it into the cave.

The Causes of a Monk's Pewter Staff

In the country of Mathurā there was a good man who became a monk at the place where Upagupta was. Upagupta preached the Dharma to him, and after having heard the Dharma the *bhikṣu* gained the four stages of worldly *dhyāna*. The *bhikṣu* thought to himself, "I have done what is to be done. There is no need to be energetic any more." Upagupta said to him, "Good man, you should be energetic; do not be lazy and negligent." The *bhikṣu* said in reply, "*Upādhyāya*, I have done what is to be done and have attained arhatship."

The *upādhyāya* ordered him to rise early in the morning, dress himself in his robes, hold his alms bowl, take up his pewter staff, and go into the presence of the monks before entering into the
169a country. There were then five hundred *upāsakas* following behind him with food and drink in their hands. Upon seeing them, the *bhikṣu* knew that they respected him, and he claimed to be a man of superior merits. Thus he had a feeling of self-conceit, and then he reflected, "I am not an arhat. An arhat is free from the conception of ego and the possession of self-conceit." So he went to the place of his *upādhyāya*, to whom he said, "I have not gained the Holy Way. May you preach the Dharma to me." Upagupta accordingly preached the Dharma to him, and through the practice of meditation the *bhikṣu* attained arhatship. Then he took a chip and put it into the cave.

The Causes of Sudarśana

In the country of Kaśmīra there was a *bhikṣu* by the name of Sudarśana who had gained the four stages of worldly *dhyāna* and was esteemed by the Nāga king. Then a drought with scorching heat occurred in the country of Kaśmīra, and all the people asked the *bhikṣu* to pray for rain. Upagupta reflected, "I wish to edify Sudarśana, and it is time now." For the sake of expedient edification, Upagupta caused that there should be no rain for twelve years, and when the heretics saw this phenomenon they said to the people, "There will be rain [only] after the lapse of twelve years." The people, being worried and distressed to hear these words, went to Upagupta and asked him to pray for rain. Upagupta said, "I should not pray for rain. In the country of Kaśmīra there is a *bhikṣu* by the name of Sudarśana, and you may go to beseech him." Then the people of Mathurā sent a messenger to Sudarśana, asking him to pray for rain. As Sudarśana possessed the miraculous powers of the four stages of *dhyāna*, he went to the country of Mathurā by divine power, and the people [again] asked him to pray for rain. Then Sudarśana prayed for rain, which poured down on the earth, filling the whole of Jambudvīpa. The people thought, "Since the *bhikṣu* Sudarśana was able to cause such a torrential rain, he is superior to Upagupta."

At that time, Sudarśana, followed by many people, was going out of the country of Mathurā, while Upagupta, followed by a few people, was coming into the country of Mathurā. When the *bhikṣu* Sudarśana saw that many people were following him while only a few people were following Upagupta, he had a feeling of self-conceit, and then he reflected, "I am not an arhat. An arhat should have no self-conceit." So he went to the place of Upagupta, and upon arriving there he worshipped at his feet and said, "The Buddha has entered nirvana. Most Virtuous One, you are performing the Buddha's functions. May you preach the Dharma to me." Upagupta said, "You are not keeping the precepts in the right way as taught by the Buddha, and you claimed superiority over me, giving rise to arrogance and self-conceit. Where did the Buddha say that he allowed his *bhikṣus* to pray for rain?" Upagupta preached the Dharma to him, and upon hearing the Dharma the *bhikṣu* diligently practiced meditation and attained arhatship. So he took a chip and put it into the cave.

169b The Causes of the Fief for a Monastery

Upagupta constructed not one but a hundred monasteries in the country of Mathurā. At that time the king of Mathurā was named Citraketu, a man who had no faith but troubled and disturbed the monks as well as their attendants and almsgivers. Then the innumerable monks together with their attendants and almsgivers went to Upagupta and told him about this matter. Upagupta reflected, "If I send a messenger to inform King Aśoka, he might be angry and would certainly kill this king. I must go in person." By miraculous power, Upagupta suddenly disappeared in a wink from Naṭabhaṭikā Monastery and reached Kukkuṭa Monastery in the city of Pāṭaliputra.

Upon hearing that Upagupta was coming, King Aśoka decorated the frontier with incense and flowers, arranged dancers and musicians with various kinds of adornment, and went with his ministers and people of the country to welcome Upagupta. When he arrived there, he worshipped at the monk's feet and, with hands joined palm to palm reverentially, said to him, "Most Virtuous One, why do you come here?" The monk said in reply, "It is for some matter that I have come to Your Majesty." The king inquired again, "What matter?" The Most Virtuous One said in reply, "Your Majesty has widely propagated the Buddha-dharma and has constructed not one but a hundred monasteries in the country of Mathurā. The reigning King Citraketu of that country has no faith but troubles and disturbs the Buddha-dharma. It befits Your Majesty to ask him to protect the Buddha-dharma." King Aśoka then ordered his minister Rādhagupta, saying, "You will dispatch a man immediately to kill that king." Upagupta said to King [Aśoka], "Do not kill that king. Let Your Majesty just instruct him not to trouble and disturb the Buddha-dharma again henceforward."

King Aśoka then wrote a letter with his own hands, marked it with his teeth, and handed it to a Rākṣasa. After taking the letter, the Rākṣasa instantly reached that country. King Citraketu received the letter respectfully and read it, and after reading the letter he struck a drum and made an announcement that thenceforth all people in the country should not trouble or disturb the Buddha-dharma.

King Aśoka inquired of Upagupta, "Which monastery has been disturbed by theft and robbery?" Upagupta said in reply, "Naṭabhaṭikā Monastery." Then King Aśoka wrote a document with his own hands to the effect that land was bestowed upon that monastery as a fief for its support. He marked it with his teeth and gave it to Upagupta. Then King Aśoka prepared various kinds of offerings, and after having accepted the offerings Upagupta suddenly disappeared from Kukkuṭa Monastery and returned to Naṭabhaṭikā Monastery.

The Causes of Dhītika

Upagupta contemplated whether Dhītika was born or not and saw
169c that he was not yet born. Thenceforth he went to the place of [Dhītika's] parents every day. One day he went to their house with many *bhikṣus*, another day he went there with only two *bhikṣus*, and on still another day he went alone. The householder, seeing that Upagupta came alone to his house, asked him, "Holy man, why do you not have any disciples following you?" The elder said in reply, "I have no disciple." The householder said, "I take delight in living at home and would not like to become a monk. If a son is born to me, I shall give him to you, Most Virtuous One, to be your disciple."

Then a son was born to the householder, but he died shortly afterwards. When the second son was born, he also died soon. When the third son was born, he was named Dhītika and given to Upagupta to become a monk. Upagupta made him a fully ordained monk. At the moment of performing the first *karman*, he attained the fruition of a *srota-āpanna*, and at the moment of performing the fourth *karman*, he attained arhatship. Upagupta reflected, "I have edified all those whom I should edify. This cave, which is eighteen cubits in length and twelve in breadth, is already filled up with chips four inches long. I should now enter nirvana."

After thinking in this way, Upagupta handed over the Dharma-*piṭaka* to Dhītika and said to him, "Good man, the World-honored One transmitted the Dharma-*piṭaka* to Mahākāśyapa and entered *parinirvāṇa*; Mahākāśyapa transmitted the Dharma-*piṭaka* to Ānanda and entered nirvana; Ānanda transmitted the Dharma-*piṭaka* to Madhyāntika and entered nirvana; Madhyāntika transmitted the Dharma-*piṭaka* to my *upādhyāya* and entered nirvana; and my *upādhyāya* transmitted the Dharma-*piṭaka* to me. Now I wish to enter nirvana; you should safeguard and protect this Dharma-*piṭaka*."

Seven days later, when Upagupta was about to enter nirvana, various heavenly beings made the matter known to all the people in the whole of Jambudvīpa, among whom there were a hundred thousand arhats, while harmonious learners, energetic ordinary *bhikṣus*, and white-clad lay people were innumerable and countless. When the time arrived for the nirvana of Upagupta, he rose up into the air by supernatural powers and made different kinds of miraculous transformations in the postures of walking, standing, sitting, and lying down. Then he entered the fire *samādhi*. When he was in the *samādhi*, various colors—blue, yellow, red, and white—issued from his body. When water flowed out from the upper part of his body, fire spurted from the lower part; when water flowed out from the lower part, fire spurted from the upper part. With various divine powers he aroused a feeling of great happiness in the minds of his fellow monks and all human and heavenly beings and enabled them to gain emancipation. Then he entered nirvana, like a fire quenched by water. The chips collected were used to cremate his body, and a stupa was built to which offerings were made.

At the time of Upagupta's nirvana, a thousand arhats also sacrificed their lives and entered nirvana. When Dhītika had safeguarded and protected the Dharma-*piṭaka*, he also entered nirvana.

170a This is the end of the *Causes of Upagupta*.

The right Dharma always abides
For a long time without dying.
The stupa containing *śarīras*
Will also last like this.
May the people who uphold the Dharma
Enjoy happiness illimitable.
May they live in the same way,
Always abiding and imperishable.

From the "Causes of King Aśoka" up to the nirvana of Upagupta, there are altogether thirty-one hundred verses, each consisting of thirty-two syllables in the foreign [text]. The number of disciples is twenty-eight persons.

Glossary

Abhidharma [*piṭaka*]: the section of the Buddhist canon containing philosophical commentaries

agrakulika: one of prominent family

airāvata: a kind of tree

āmra: mango

anāgāmin: one never to be reborn on this earth

apsaras: a kind of goddess

arhat: one who has attained nirvana

ariṣṭaka: heron

Asura: a kind of demon, an evil spirit

āyatana: entrance

bakula: a kind of flower

bhikṣu: Buddhist monk

bhikṣuṇī: Buddhist nun

bodhisattva: one destined for enlightenment

caitya: shrine

cakravartin: universal monarch; emperor of the earth

caṇḍāla: outcaste; wicked, butcher

caṇḍālī: outcaste (f.)

Deva: god

dhāraṇī: incantation

Dharmakāya: body of truth

Dharma-*piṭaka*: collection of Buddhist texts

Dharmarāja: a Buddhist king

dhātu: sphere

dhyāna: trance

duṣkṛta: misdeed or sin

eight precepts: (1) not to kill, (2) not to steal, (3) not to commit adultery, (4) not to speak falsely, (5) not to drink intoxicants, (6) not to sing, dance, or wear ornaments, (7) not to sit or sleep on a high bed, and (8) not to eat after noon.

Elder: Buddhist monk of many years' standing

four noble truths: (1) life is suffering; (2) defilements are the cause of suffering; (3) all suffering can be ended; (4) the way to end suffering is the eightfold noble path (i.e., right view, right thought, right speech, right action, right livelihood, right effort, right mindfulness, and right concentration)

gandha-jala: fragrant water

gāthā: stanza

hetupratyaya: cause and subcause

jambu: a kind of tree

Jambudvīpa: the world

Jātaka stories: tales of the Buddha's previous lives as a bodhisattva

jāti: rebirth

jhāpita: cremation

kadamba: a kind of flower, *Nandea cadamba*

kalpa: immense period of time, aeon

Kāmadhātu: realm of desire

karma: the consequences of a person's past actions

karmadāna: distributor of duties

karman: act of the ordination ceremony

Kṣatriya: governmental caste, warrior caste; one of this caste

kulika: one of good family

kumuda: red lotus

Kuṇāla: Aśoka's son

kuṇāla: a kind of bird

kuṅkuma: turmeric

kuṭaru-navaka: new tent

lākṣā: red dye

lakuca: glue

mallikā: jasmine

mandārava: a kind of flower

maṇi: pearl

Māra: demon

mātṛkā: See Abhidharma [*piṭaka*]

Nāga: dragon

niṣīdana: mat for sitting

pārājika: "defeat," ground for expulsion from the Sangha

pātra: alms bowl

pippalī: a long pepper

piṭaka: collection of Buddhist texts

pratyekabuddha: self-enlightened Buddha

puṇḍarīka: white lotus

Rākṣasa: a kind of demon

Rūpakāya: physical body of a Buddha

sakṛdāgāmin: one who will return to the world once more before enlightenment

samādhi: deep trance

saṃghāṭī robe: outer robe

śāṇa: hempen (garment)

śāṇavāsa: hempen garment

Sangha: Buddhist Order

śarīra: relic

six *pāramitā*s: six perfected virtues concerning giving, precept-keeping, patience, effort, meditation, and wisdom

*skandha*s: aggregates

śramaṇa: Buddhist monk

śrāvaka: "hearer," personal disciple of the Buddha

srota-āpanna: one who has "entered the stream" of contemplation

stupa: tope, reliquary

Sugata: the Buddha ("well-gone")

Sutra: a discourse of the Buddha

tāla: leaf

Tripiṭaka: Buddhist canon

Udāna and *Gāthā*: sections of the Buddhist canon

upādhyāya: teacher

upāsaka: layman

upāsikā: laywoman

utpala: blue lotus

Vinaya: Buddhist monastic rules

Yakṣa: a kind of devil

yojana: one day's journey in an ox cart

Index

Niṣīdana, 100
Non-action, 23
Non-ego, 6, 158
Novices, 48

Padmāvatī (Aśoka's wife), 63
Pārājika(s), 102
Pāramitās. *See* Six *Pāramitās*
Parthia, 1
Pāṭaliputra (city), 1, 7–9, 11, 15, 17, 23, 56, 88, 181
Pātra, 110
Physiognomist, 8–10, 29, 66, 70
Piṇḍavana (monastery), 124
Piṇḍola Bhāradvāja (elder), 42–45, 47
Piṅgalavatsājīva (heretical physiognomist), 9
Pippalī, 68
Pippalāyana Grotto, 99, 112
Piṭaka(s). *See* Tripiṭaka
Pratyekabuddha(s), 6, 42, 60, 77, 92, 93, 125, 151
Precept(s), 88, 115, 125, 126, 181
  Eight, 41
Prince(s), 9–12, 15, 46, 47, 49–52, 67, 69, 75, 76, 82, 83, 87, 119
Provisor, 159, 160
Puṇḍarīka, 122, 126
Puṇḍravardhana (country), 44
Puṇyavardhana (country), 58, 59
Pūrṇa (elder), 96, 97
Puṣyamitra (king), 1, 87–89

Qi dynasty, 2

Rādhagupta (Aśoka's minister), 9, 12, 13, 45, 46, 82, 86, 87, 182
Raft, 94, 134
Rājagṛha (city), 3, 43, 45, 98, 99, 109, 111, 113, 118, 122
Rākṣasa(s), 113, 164, 182
Rāmagrāma (village), 19
Realms, three, 16, 17, 23, 53, 74, 100, 101, 168
Rebirth/Reincarnation, 6, 26, 29, 33, 35, 55, 74, 94, 116, 134, 147, 148, 153, 157, 159, 161, 163, 165, 167, 168, 172, 173
Recluse(s), 6, 8, 16, 25, 29, 30, 33, 70, 92, 101, 114, 117, 119–21, 141
Relic(s), 17–21, 25, 34, 41, 45, 94, 109
  bones, 7, 8
  hair and nail, 61
  stupas, 38, 110
  tooth, 88, 89, 110
Rūpakāya, 141

Ṣāgara (monk), 15
Śakra, 33, 35, 86, 93–95, 110, 112, 137, 138
Sakṛdāgāmin, 121, 145, 154, 174, 175, 177
Śākyamuni, 15, 49, 50, 80, 94, 114, 168, 172
Sālā (country), 139
Sāla (tree), 94
Samādhi, 57, 102, 109, 121, 136, 146, 150–52, 184
  of cessation, 108
  of compassion, 122, 123, 126, 127
  fire, 121, 152, 156, 184
  five kinds of, 146
  of non-disputation, 43
  as Powerful as a Dragon, 150
  of Pure Harmony and the [Seven] Phases of Enlightenment, 151
  of suchness, 122
Saṃghāṭī, 114
Sāṃkāśya (country), 44
Ṣaṃpadin (Kuṇāla's son), 82, 87
Śāṇa, 109, 115, 146
Śāṇakavāsin (fourth patriarch), 2, 91, 107, 109, 114, 115, 118, 124–29, 135, 146, 149–52
Śāṇavāsa, 125, 126
Sand, offering of, 5, 7, 8, 21, 26, 45, 82
Sangha, 18, 42, 47, 53, 54, 60, 70, 81, 85–87, 96, 97, 99, 134, 135, 171
Śāriputra (elder), 34, 115, 117, 142, 151
Śarīra, 41, 124, 184
Sarvamitra (monk), 46
Sects, five, 40, 46, 47, 49
Self-enlightened Buddha. See *Pratyekabuddha*
Śirīṣa Palace, 95, 96
Six *pāramitā*s, 143
*Skandha*s, 153
  five, 53
Skeleton, 133, 170
Snow Mountains, 64, 79, 120
South Sea, 89

A List of the Volumes of the BDK English Tripiṭaka (First Series)

Abbreviations

Ch.: Chinese
Skt.: Sanskrit
Jp.: Japanese
T.: Taishō Tripiṭaka

Vol. No.		Title	*T.* No.
1, 2	*Ch.*	Ch'ang-a-han-ching (長阿含經)	1
	Skt.	Dīrghāgama	
3–8	*Ch.*	Chung-a-han-ching (中阿含經)	26
	Skt.	Madhyamāgama	
9-I	*Ch.*	Ta-ch'eng-pên-shêng-hsin-ti-kuan-ching (大乘本生心地觀經)	159
9-II	*Ch.*	Fo-so-hsing-tsan (佛所行讃)	192
	Skt.	Buddhacarita	
10-I	*Ch.*	Tsa-pao-ts'ang-ching (雜寶藏經)	203
10-II	*Ch.*	Fa-chü-p'i-yü-ching (法句譬喩經)	211
11-I	*Ch.*	Hsiao-p'in-pan-jo-po-lo-mi-ching (小品般若波羅蜜經)	227
	Skt.	Aṣṭasāhasrikā-prajñāpāramitā-sūtra	
11-II	*Ch.*	Chin-kang-pan-jo-po-lo-mi-ching (金剛般若波羅蜜經)	235
	Skt.	Vajracchedikā-prajñāpāramitā-sūtra	

Vol. No.		Title	T. No.
11-III	*Ch.*	Jên-wang-pan-jo-po-lo-mi-ching (仁王般若波羅蜜經)	245
	Skt.	Kāruṇikārājā-prajñāpāramitā-sūtra (?)	
11-IV	*Ch.*	Pan-jo-po-lo-mi-to-hsing-ching (般若波羅蜜多心經)	251
	Skt.	Prajñāpāramitāhṛdaya-sūtra	
12-I	*Ch.*	Ta-lo-chin-kang-pu-k'ung-chên-shih-san-mo-yeh-ching (大樂金剛不空眞實三麼耶經)	243
	Skt.	Adhyardhaśatikā-prajñāpāramitā-sūtra	
12-II	*Ch.*	Wu-liang-shou-ching (無量壽經)	360
	Skt.	Sukhāvatīvyūha	
12-III	*Ch.*	Kuan-wu-liang-shou-fo-ching (觀無量壽佛經)	365
	Skt.	Amitāyurdhyāna-sūtra	
12-IV	*Ch.*	A-mi-t'o-ching (阿彌陀經)	366
	Skt.	Sukhāvatīvyūha	
12-V	*Ch.*	Ti-ts'ang-p'u-sa-pên-yüan-ching (地藏菩薩本願經)	412
	Skt.	Kṣitigarbhapraṇidhāna-sūtra (?)	
12-VI	*Ch.*	Yao-shih-liu-li-kuang-ju-lai-pên-yüan-kung-tê-ching (藥師琉璃光如來本願功德經)	450
	Skt.	Bhaiṣajyaguruvaiḍūryaprabhāsapūrvapraṇidhānaviśeṣavistara	
12-VII	*Ch.*	Mi-lê-hsia-shêng-ch'êng-fo-ching (彌勒下生成佛經)	454
	Skt.	Maitreyavyākaraṇa (?)	
12-VIII	*Ch.*	Wên-shu-shih-li-wên-ching (文殊師利問經)	468
	Skt.	Mañjuśrīparipṛcchā (?)	
13-I	*Ch.*	Miao-fa-lien-hua-ching (妙法蓮華經)	262
	Skt.	Saddharmapuṇḍarīka-sūtra	
13-II	*Ch.*	Wu-liang-i-ching (無量義經)	276
13-III	*Ch.*	Kuan-p'u-hsien-p'u-sa-hsing-fa-ching (觀普賢菩薩行法經)	277
14–19	*Ch.*	Ta-fang-kuang-fo-hua-yen-ching (大方廣佛華嚴經)	278
	Skt.	Avataṃsaka-sūtra	

Vol. No.		Title	T. No.
20-I	*Ch.*	Shêng-man-shih-tzŭ-hou-i-ch'eng-ta-fang-pien-fang-kuang-ching (勝鬘師子吼一乘大方便方廣經)	353
	Skt.	Śrīmālādevīsiṃhanāda-sūtra	
20-II	*Ch.*	Chin-kuang-ming-tsui-shêng-wang-ching (金光明最勝王經)	665
	Skt.	Suvarṇaprabhāsa-sūtra	
21–24	*Ch.*	Ta-pan-nieh-p'an-ching (大般涅槃經)	374
	Skt.	Mahāparinirvāṇa-sūtra	
25-I	*Ch.*	Fo-ch'ui-pan-nieh-p'an-liao-shuo-chiao-chieh-ching (佛垂般涅槃略説教誡經)	389
25-II	*Ch.*	Pan-chou-san-mei-ching (般舟三昧經)	418
	Skt.	Pratyutpannabuddhasammukhāvasthitasamādhi-sūtra	
25-III	*Ch.*	Shou-lêng-yen-san-mei-ching (首楞嚴三昧經)	642
	Skt.	Śūraṅgamasamādhi-sūtra	
25-IV	*Ch.*	Chieh-shên-mi-ching (解深密經)	676
	Skt.	Saṃdhinirmocana-sūtra	
25-V	*Ch.*	Yü-lan-p'ên-ching (盂蘭盆經)	685
	Skt.	Ullambana-sūtra (?)	
25-VI	*Ch.*	Ssŭ-shih-êrh-chang-ching (四十二章經)	784
26-I	*Ch.*	Wei-mo-chieh-so-shuo-ching (維摩詰所説經)	475
	Skt.	Vimalakīrtinirdeśa-sūtra	
26-II	*Ch.*	Yüeh-shang-nü-ching (月上女經)	480
	Skt.	Candrottarādārikāparipṛcchā	
26-III	*Ch.*	Tso-ch'an-san-mei-ching (坐禪三昧經)	614
26-IV	*Ch.*	Ta-mo-to-lo-ch'an-ching (達摩多羅禪經)	618
	Skt.	Yogācārabhūmi-sūtra (?)	
27	*Ch.*	Yüeh-têng-san-mei-ching (月燈三昧經)	639
	Skt.	Samādhirājacandrapradīpa-sūtra	
28	*Ch.*	Ju-lêng-ch'ieh-ching (入楞伽經)	671
	Skt.	Laṅkāvatāra-sūtra	

Vol. No.		Title	T. No.
29-I	*Ch.*	Ta-fang-kuang-yüan-chio-hsiu-to-lo-liao-i-ching (大方廣圓覺修多羅了義經)	842
29-II	*Ch.*	Su-hsi-ti-chieh-lo-ching (蘇悉地羯羅經)	893
	Skt.	Susiddhikaramahātantrasādhanopāyika-paṭala	
29-III	*Ch.*	Mo-têng-ch'ieh-ching (摩登伽經)	1300
	Skt.	Mātaṅgī-sūtra (?)	
30-I	*Ch.*	Ta-p'i-lu-chê-na-ch'êng-fo-shên-pien-chia-ch'ih-ching (大毘盧遮那成佛神變加持經)	848
	Skt.	Mahāvairocanābhisambodhivikurvitādhiṣṭhāna-vaipulyasūtrendrarāja-nāma-dharmaparyāya	
30-II	*Ch.*	Chin-kang-ting-i-ch'ieh-ju-lai-chên-shih-shê-ta-ch'eng-hsien-chêng-ta-chiao-wang-ching (金剛頂一切如來眞實攝大乘現證大教王經)	865
	Skt.	Sarvatathāgatatattvasaṃgrahamahāyānābhi-samayamahākalparāja	
31–35	*Ch.*	Mo-ho-sêng-ch'i-lü (摩訶僧祇律)	1425
	Skt.	Mahāsāṃghika-vinaya (?)	
36–42	*Ch.*	Ssŭ-fên-lü (四分律)	1428
	Skt.	Dharmaguptaka-vinaya (?)	
43, 44	*Ch.*	Shan-chien-lü-p'i-p'o-sha (善見律毘婆沙)	1462
	Pāli	Samantapāsādikā	
45-I	*Ch.*	Fan-wang-ching (梵網經)	1484
	Skt.	Brahmajāla-sūtra (?)	
45-II	*Ch.*	Yu-p'o-sai-chieh-ching (優婆塞戒經)	1488
	Skt.	Upāsakaśīla-sūtra (?)	
46-I	*Ch.*	Miao-fa-lien-hua-ching-yu-po-t'i-shê (妙法蓮華經憂波提舍)	1519
	Skt.	Saddharmapuṇḍarīkopadeśa	
46-II	*Ch.*	Fo-ti-ching-lun (佛地經論)	1530
	Skt.	Buddhabhūmisūtra-śāstra (?)	
46-III	*Ch.*	Shê-ta-ch'eng-lun (攝大乘論)	1593
	Skt.	Mahāyānasaṃgraha	
47	*Ch.*	Shih-chu-p'i-p'o-sha-lun (十住毘婆沙論)	1521
	Skt.	Daśabhūmika-vibhāṣā (?)	

Vol. No.		Title	T. No.
48, 49	*Ch.*	A-p'i-ta-mo-chü-shê-lun (阿毘達磨俱舍論)	1558
	Skt.	Abhidharmakośa-bhāṣya	
50–59	*Ch.*	Yü-ch'ieh-shih-ti-lun (瑜伽師地論)	1579
	Skt.	Yogācārabhūmi	
60-I	*Ch.*	Ch'êng-wei-shih-lun (成唯識論)	1585
	Skt.	Vijñaptimātratāsiddhi-śāstra (?)	
60-II	*Ch.*	Wei-shih-san-shih-lun-sung (唯識三十論頌)	1586
	Skt.	Triṃśikā	
60-III	*Ch.*	Wei-shih-êrh-shih-lun (唯識二十論)	1590
	Skt.	Viṃśatikā	
61-I	*Ch.*	Chung-lun (中論)	1564
	Skt.	Madhyamaka-śāstra	
61-II	*Ch.*	Pien-chung-pien-lun (辯中邊論)	1600
	Skt.	Madhyāntavibhāga	
61-III	*Ch.*	Ta-ch'eng-ch'êng-yeh-lun (大乘成業論)	1609
	Skt.	Karmasiddhiprakaraṇa	
61-IV	*Ch.*	Yin-ming-ju-chêng-li-lun (因明入正理論)	1630
	Skt.	Nyāyapraveśa	
61-V	*Ch.*	Chin-kang-chên-lun (金剛針論)	1642
	Skt.	Vajrasūcī	
61-VI	*Ch.*	Chang-so-chih-lun (彰所知論)	1645
62	*Ch.*	Ta-ch'eng-chuang-yen-ching-lun (大乘莊嚴經論)	1604
	Skt.	Mahāyānasūtrālaṃkāra	
63-I	*Ch.*	Chiu-ching-i-ch'eng-pao-hsing-lun (究竟一乘寶性論)	1611
	Skt.	Ratnagotravibhāgamahāyānottaratantra-śāstra	
63-II	*Ch.*	P'u-t'i-hsing-ching (菩提行經)	1662
	Skt.	Bodhicaryāvatāra	
63-III	*Ch.*	Chin-kang-ting-yü-ch'ieh-chung-fa-a-nou-to-lo-san-miao-san-p'u-t'i-hsin-lun (金剛頂瑜伽中發阿耨多羅三藐三菩提心論)	1665
63-IV	*Ch.*	Ta-ch'eng-ch'i-hsin-lun (大乘起信論)	1666
	Skt.	Mahāyānaśraddhotpāda-śāstra (?)	

Vol. No.		Title	*T.* No.
63-V	*Ch.* *Pāli*	Na-hsien-pi-ch'iu-ching (那先比丘經) Milindapañhā	1670
64	*Ch.* *Skt.*	Ṭa-ch'eng-chi-p'u-sa-hsüeh-lun (大乘集菩薩學論) Śikṣāsamuccaya	1636
65	*Ch.*	Shih-mo-ho-yen-lun (釋摩訶衍論)	1668
66-I	*Ch.*	Pan-jo-po-lo-mi-to-hsin-ching-yu-tsan (般若波羅蜜多心經幽賛)	1710
66-II	*Ch.*	Kuan-wu-liang-shou-fo-ching-shu (觀無量壽佛經疏)	1753
66-III	*Ch.*	San-lun-hsüan-i (三論玄義)	1852
66-IV	*Ch.*	Chao-lun (肇論)	1858
67, 68	*Ch.*	Miao-fa-lien-hua-ching-hsüan-i (妙法蓮華經玄義)	1716
69	*Ch.*	Ta-ch'eng-hsüan-lun (大乘玄論)	1853
70-I	*Ch.*	Hua-yen-i-ch'eng-chiao-i-fên-ch'i-chang (華嚴一乘教義分齊章)	1866
70-II	*Ch.*	Yüan-jên-lun (原人論)	1886
70-III	*Ch.*	Hsiu-hsi-chih-kuan-tso-ch'an-fa-yao (修習止觀坐禪法要)	1915
70-IV	*Ch.*	T'ien-t'ai-ssŭ-chiao-i (天台四教儀)	1931
71, 72	*Ch.*	Mo-ho-chih-kuan (摩訶止觀)	1911
73-I	*Ch.*	Kuo-ch'ing-pai-lu (國清百録)	1934
73-II	*Ch.*	Liu-tsu-ta-shih-fa-pao-t'an-ching (六祖大師法寶壇經)	2008
73-III	*Ch.*	Huang-po-shan-tuan-chi-ch'an-shih-ch'uan-hsin-fa-yao (黄檗山斷際禪師傳心法要)	2012 A
73-IV	*Ch.*	Yung-chia-chêng-tao-ko (永嘉證道歌)	2014
74-I	*Ch.*	Chên-chou-lin-chi-hui-chao-ch'an-shih-wu-lu (鎭州臨濟慧照禪師語録)	1985
74-II	*Ch.*	Wu-mên-kuan (無門關)	2005

Vol. No.		Title	T. No.
74-III	*Ch.*	Hsin-hsin-ming (信心銘)	2010
74-IV	*Ch.*	Ch'ih-hsiu-pai-chang-ch'ing-kuei (勅修百丈清規)	2025
75	*Ch.*	Fo-kuo-yüan-wu-ch'an-shih-pi-yen-lu (佛果圜悟禪師碧巖録)	2003
76-I	*Ch.* *Skt.*	I-pu-tsung-lun-lun (異部宗輪論) Samayabhedoparacanacakra	2031
76-II	*Ch.* *Skt.*	A-yü-wang-ching (阿育王經) Aśokarāja-sūtra (?)	2043
76-III	*Ch.*	Ma-ming-p'u-sa-ch'uan (馬鳴菩薩傳)	2046
76-IV	*Ch.*	Lung-shu-p'u-sa-ch'uan (龍樹菩薩傳)	2047
76-V	*Ch.*	P'o-sou-p'an-tou-fa-shih-ch'uan (婆藪槃豆法師傳)	2049
76-VI	*Ch.*	Pi-ch'iu-ni-ch'uan (比丘尼傳)	2063
76-VII	*Ch.*	Kao-sêng-fa-hsien-ch'uan (高僧法顯傳)	2085
76-VIII	*Ch.*	T'ang-ta-ho-shang-tung-chêng-ch'uan (遊方記抄:唐大和上東征傳)	2089-(7)
77	*Ch.*	Ta-t'ang-ta-tz'ŭ-ên-ssŭ-san-ts'ang-fa-shih-ch'uan (大唐大慈恩寺三藏法師傳)	2053
78	*Ch.*	Kao-sêng-ch'uan (高僧傳)	2059
79	*Ch.*	Ta-t'ang-hsi-yü-chi (大唐西域記)	2087
80	*Ch.*	Hung-ming-chi (弘明集)	2102
81–92	*Ch.*	Fa-yüan-chu-lin (法苑珠林)	2122
93-I	*Ch.*	Nan-hai-chi-kuei-nei-fa-ch'uan (南海寄歸内法傳)	2125
93-II	*Ch.*	Fan-yü-tsa-ming (梵語雜名)	2135
94-I	*Jp.*	Shō-man-gyō-gi-sho (勝鬘經義疏)	2185
94-II	*Jp.*	Yui-ma-kyō-gi-sho (維摩經義疏)	2186
95	*Jp.*	Hok-ke-gi-sho (法華義疏)	2187

Vol. No.		Title	*T.* No.
96-I	*Jp.*	Han-nya-shin-gyō-hi-ken (般若心經秘鍵)	2203
96-II	*Jp.*	Dai-jō-hos-sō-ken-jin-shō (大乘法相研神章)	2309
96-III	*Jp.*	Kan-jin-kaku-mu-shō (觀心覺夢鈔)	2312
97-I	*Jp.*	Ris-shū-kō-yō (律宗綱要)	2348
97-II	*Jp.*	Ten-dai-hok-ke-shū-gi-shū (天台法華宗義集)	2366
97-III	*Jp.*	Ken-kai-ron (顯戒論)	2376
97-IV	*Jp.*	San-ge-gaku-shō-shiki (山家學生式)	2377
98-I	*Jp.*	Hi-zō-hō-yaku (秘藏寶鑰)	2426
98-II	*Jp.*	Ben-ken-mitsu-ni-kyō-ron (辨顯密二教論)	2427
98-III	*Jp.*	Soku-shin-jō-butsu-gi (即身成佛義)	2428
98-IV	*Jp.*	Shō-ji-jis-sō-gi (聲字實相義)	2429
98-V	*Jp.*	Un-ji-gi (吽字義)	2430
98-VI	*Jp.*	Go-rin-ku-ji-myō-hi-mitsu-shaku (五輪九字明秘密釋)	2514
98-VII	*Jp.*	Mitsu-gon-in-hotsu-ro-san-ge-mon (密嚴院發露懺悔文)	2527
98-VIII	*Jp.*	Kō-zen-go-koku-ron (興禪護國論)	2543
98-IX	*Jp.*	Fu-kan-za-zen-gi (普勧坐禪儀)	2580
99–103	*Jp.*	Shō-bō-gen-zō (正法眼藏)	2582
104-I	*Jp.*	Za-zen-yō-jin-ki (坐禪用心記)	2586
104-II	*Jp.*	Sen-chaku-hon-gan-nen-butsu-shū (選擇本願念佛集)	2608
104-III	*Jp.*	Ris-shō-an-koku-ron (立正安國論)	2688
104-IV	*Jp.*	Kai-moku-shō (開目抄)	2689
104-V	*Jp.*	Kan-jin-hon-zon-shō (觀心本尊抄)	2692
104-VI	*Ch.*	Fu-mu-ên-chung-ching (父母恩重經)	2887

Vol. No.		Title	*T.* No.
105-I	*Jp.*	Ken-jō-do-shin-jitsu-kyō-gyō-shō-mon-rui (顯淨土眞實教行証文類)	2646
105-II	*Jp.*	Tan-ni-shō (歎異抄)	2661
106-I	*Jp.*	Ren-nyo-shō-nin-o-fumi (蓮如上人御文)	2668
106-II	*Jp.*	Ō-jō-yō-shū (往生要集)	2682
107-I	*Jp.*	Has-shū-kō-yō (八宗綱要)	蔵外
107-II	*Jp.*	San-gō-shī-ki (三教指帰)	蔵外
107-III	*Jp.*	Map-pō-tō-myō-ki (末法燈明記)	蔵外
107-IV	*Jp.*	Jū-shichi-jō-ken-pō (十七條憲法)	蔵外